MW00936838

HAPPINESS
for the Practical Mind

7 Steps to Discovering and Loving Your Authentic Self

❧

Jared Akers

Disclaimer: The use of this material is not a substitute for health or professional services. Consult competent professionals to answer specific questions about depression or other specific health- and wellness-related questions. If you suffer or believe you may be suffering from depression or any other emotional disorder, I encourage you to seek help from a trained mental health professional such as a psychiatrist, clinical psychologist, or licensed counselor.

Copyright and distribution notice: You are welcome and encouraged to freely distribute this document in its entirety to any and all people whom you believe would be interested in it. However, this document may not be sold for profit or any other type of commercial gain.

The contents of this document are the intellectual property of Jared Akers and Serene Horizons, LLC. However, you are welcome and encouraged to quote any material contained herein in your own published works without having to request permission. All I ask is that you credit me (Jared Akers) and provide a link back to http://jaredakers.com/ in any citations.

Happiness for the Practical Mind: 7 Steps to Discovering and Loving Your Authentic Self by Jared Akers is licensed under a Creative Commons Attribution-NonCommercial-NoDerivs 3.0 Unported License. Based on a work at jaredakers.com. Permissions beyond the scope of this license may be available at http://jaredakers.com.

© 2012 Jared Akers
All Rights Reserved.

ISBN-10: 1468163264
ISBN-13: 9781468163261

What Others Are Saying About This Book

"Happiness for the Practical Mind is a comprehensive, action-oriented guide of ideas to create happiness from the inside out, from a man who has battled his fair share of demons. It's honest, simple, and concise--a great read!"
- *Lori Deschene, Author of Tiny Buddha, Simple Wisdom for Life's Hard Questions & Founder of Tinybuddha.com*

"Happiness shouldn't be allusive, and indeed is within your reach, if you follow the steps laid out in Happiness for the Practical Mind. Jared tells you not only how to find Happiness but also how to sustain it."
- *Justin Lukasavige, Storywriter (coachradio.tv)*

"Happiness for the Practical Mind is an actionable guide that is raw, inspiring and transitional. Jared's transparent real-life journey walks you from the depths of darkness to the light, in such a way that anyone can follow it and reclaim their life and happiness. A must read for anyone serious about discovering who they are and how to be happy."
- *Laura Lake, Author of Consumer Behavior for Dummies, Marketing Columnist for About.com*

"Happiness for the Practical Mind is a valuable blueprint for sustained happiness. Jared Akers has created a book that delivers not only fascinating insights into how the mind creates feelings of happiness, it also gives excellent practical advice on how to feel more upbeat."

- *Mary Jaksch Goodlife ZEN (GoodLifeZen.com)*

This book is dedicated to my mother
Take your time & count to five...
Keep yourself always safe & alive...
The greatest gift a child can give...
Is that their parents they outlive...

Table of Contents

Preface

"All that depresses you, all that you fear, is really powerless to harm you. These things are but phantoms. So arise from earth's bonds, from depression, distrust, fear, and all that hinders your new life. Arise to beauty, joy, peace, and work inspired by love. Rise from death to life. You do not even need to fear death. All past sins are forgiven if you live and love and work with God. Let nothing hinder your new life. Seek more and more to know this new way of living."

——*Twenty-Four Hours A Day: Hazelden*

This book is my work inspired by love. Not too long ago I was at a bottom emotionally, spiritually, and physically. On March 12, 2006, I faced a difficult decision: whether or not to commit suicide. I share this not to be dramatic, invoke an emotional response, or seek attention; it's simply the way it was. It's part of my story, and it's all I have. How I got to that point in my life is not as important as what I did to move past it and find true inner-peace and happiness. It wasn't easy.

The decision I made was to pick up my phone and hit #1 on the keypad—my sister's speed dial number. Thank God she answered. "I choose life," I said. "I can't do this anymore." At that moment I asked for help and dedicated my life to finding happiness and inner-peace. Since that day I have sought therapy and spiritual counseling, read books, studied theories on happiness, and taken massive action to find true serenity, happiness, and my authentic self.

First things first—thank you so much for purchasing this book. I've spent hundreds of hours over several years writing, researching, and putting into practice everything within these pages. What you'll find here are words written purely from love, love for self and you reading this right now. What I share has come from years of experience and tremendous emotional pain. I had to do a million things perfectly wrong to get to this moment I'm in right now. I am truly grateful since I get to share what I've learned about finding happiness and inner-peace with you. And that gives me great joy, peace of mind, and happiness.

Yes, happiness can be subjective, but what I have discovered transcends all beliefs and backgrounds. A happiness that is not contingent on our past or what we may or may not accomplish in the future. I've not only experienced but witnessed this happiness in the lives of others and discovered what they have in common. Yet more importantly, this happiness is accessible to anyone. This book is what I have learned. Read it, use it, practice it, and most importantly, take action on the practical and simple keys, steps, and suggestions you find within. I say simple, not comfortable.

The keys, steps, and concepts I've put into this book have come from many different sources. There aren't a lot of new things under the sun. Many have been said before, written about, practiced, preached, and studied. It is not my intention to remake anything, just share my experience as it has worked for me. In finding happiness I've used everything at my disposal, including books, coaches, clergy, twelve-step programs, therapists, spiritual advisors, mentors, and anything else I thought would help. What I've learned centers around seven steps I have identified in myself and others that have contributed to a sustained happiness in life. The most important part of the journey towards discovering and loving our authentic self is action.

Without action, nothing is going to change. You can read all the books on self-improvement and happiness in the world (including this one), but if you take no action on what you read, you're going to continue to get the same thing out of life. If you want to experience something new and amazing—something you've never had—you have to be willing to step outside your comfort zone and take action even when it feels uncomfortable. Rhetoric rarely satisfies the soul.

Every amazing experience and the progress I've made towards happiness has been a result of action I have taken, action that puts me in direct interaction with the universe and those around me, thus providing feedback, joy, love, and happiness.

Three frogs are sitting on a log;
one decides to jump. How many are left?
Three. The one only made a decision to jump,
yet he took no action.

What Makes This Book Different Than All The Others?

What frustrates me more than anything is all the advice people out there are giving about how to be happy. Things like: be grateful, live in the now, surrender, stop judging others, lower expectations, do what you love, follow your passions, help someone else, blah, blah, blah. It's all the same thing just said in different ways. And although I agree *these are all important keys to happiness,* we've heard it already, we know! My question was: how do I stop judging others or lower expectations? Huh? How exactly do I do that? Show me! I need pictures or stick figures, drawings, diagrams, or exercises…something, anything! Throw me a friggin' bone, people!

No matter what you do or achieve in your lifetime, if you're not happy with yourself, nothing is going to bring you happiness. Period.

I don't know about you, but I can be...well, *slow* sometimes. I need examples and practical ways of learning a lesson. I need someone to say, "To learn surrender, rake your neighbor's yard when they're away regardless of how hectic and time-constrained you 'think' your life is. Oh, and do it anonymously."

That's what this book is: a practical guide of actions that, if followed, will result in a happier, more peaceful way of living. I guarantee that if you follow the keys, steps, and suggestions in this book, your life *will* change.

I've worked (and continue to work) through each of the steps listed in this book. Some take longer than others. For me, the initial process of working through everything outlined in this book took approximately nine months. After that, it's all just maintenance. It's still a little work, but it's a heck of a lot easier staying happy then getting happy.

Before we get into changing your life, there are a few requirements *cough* I mean, suggestions, to keep in mind while reading.

Firstly, keep an open mind. Everything I share and have learned is from personal experience as well as people I have witnessed who have found happiness, inner-peace, and serenity in their lives through actions they have taken. Listen for the similarities and not the differences as you read. Specifically, identify with the feelings, emotions, and fears.

"The mind is like a parachute——it works only when it is open."

— Frank Zappa

Secondly, what translates to happiness for one person may not be the same for the next. However, inner-peace through discovering and loving your authentic self is universal, and, as you'll discover, leads to happiness. Moreover, regardless of background or personal history, people from all types have found inner-peace and happiness by changing the way they think——about themselves and the world around them. Again, I only ask that you keep an open mind. I say this because I struggled for years with what I perceived happiness to be. I discovered *why* I continued to fail at sustaining long-term inner-peace and happiness; I was chasing the wrong things. Just keep that in mind as you read through this book.

A victim is a spectator in his or her own life. **This book officially gives you permission to stop being a victim**. Regardless of what has or has not happened in your past, you can move beyond it and begin participating in your own life. The process is simple but not easy. During the journey, always remember one important thing: if it feels uncomfortable, it's working.

I am six years old and shivering as I glare at the freezing water from the edge of a pool. Its 7:30 a.m.——I'm supposed to be in the water with the rest of the students…and my mother. Scared and cold, I muster every bit of courage I have, and jump.

A few short minutes later, I am okay. Actually, the water feels good now, not nearly as cold as when I jumped in. Did the water temperature change? Of course not—the water temperature did not change; I did.

> —The Secret About: Change and Spiritual Growth,
> Jared Akers / JaredAkers.com

Come on in, the water is fine!

Prologue

After a failed marriage, a lost job, and a friend who had recently passed away, I was depressed and overwhelmed with life. From a loft apartment in downtown Kansas City, Missouri, I would make my final stand. With money in the bank and a liquor store three blocks away, I was in heaven, and hell. This is how I remember those last few days.

March 12, 2006, 12:45 a.m.

Eight hundred pounds, my body, my soul, weighs eight hundred pounds. For days, I have been laying here on this futon, alone in this loft, too weak to walk or eat much. The booze has stopped working. The empty bottles are a reminder of what is left of my soul, emptiness. Every warm drop of life sucked out of them. I remember hearing that personal hygiene is one of the first things to go as we totally lose control and go insane. For the last few days, I have forced myself to crawl the twenty feet to the bathtub.

Not any more; I don't care. My fingernails are long. I used to hate that.

There is a pipe running through my loft about eight feet from the floor. The paint is chipped and peeling. The smooth outer shell that once hid its cold hard underneath, enabling it to blend in with its surroundings, is falling away. In the corner, a half-built entertainment center, my thirty-two-inch hi-def TV sits on the floor. Next to it, a pair of component video cables; I will use those to hang myself from the pipe. How fitting to kill the *monster* I have become inside. It's going to be epic; my story will touch the lives of others and give them the strength I lack. Maybe I should get a video camera and film my own demise… I'll be famous. Who am I kidding? I'm too weak to even walk two blocks to the store, and my car has two flat tires and tags that have been expired for a year and a half. I would never make it.

Strewn about the loft is evidence of my last days here. Several dozen empty vodka bottles—more hidden in the empty cabinets—as many empty beer bottles, a pile of unpaid bills, dirty clothes, sunflower seeds, empty pizza boxes, and one of those single sandwich grills where I cook frozen hamburger patties to force-feed myself.

A blanket covers the window, making it hard to distinguish night from day. Paranoia insisted I cover the peephole in the door, and pillows line the small closet where I spend most daylight hours in case someone tries to enter. On the street below, iron sheets cover holes in the street—unfinished work to be done. Cars passing randomly, "thump-thump," add to my paranoia. Was someone knocking? From my latest count, there are 530 bricks along the north wall. That can't be right; it's a big wall. I lose concentration. I am going crazy.

Growing up, my mother would say, "The greatest gift a child can give is that their parents they outlive." She hasn't come to see me. My father came last week to see how I was doing. He left with tears in his eyes when I told him everything was going to be okay; his response, "It's *not* okay, son."

My parents live about an hour away. For my father to come to the "big city" says a lot. I don't think he has ever been here before. I wonder how he found me. A cousin of mine came by, too, as well as some friends; I sent them all away. Even the police responded to a call about my well-being; they thought I was on meth—geesh, can't they tell a drunken crazy man when they see one? As with everyone, I sent them away, "I'm fine." But not before thanking them and telling them everything was going to be okay, that this was my decision and I'm okay with it. I was more concerned for their conscience, that it be void of any regrets that they didn't try something.

Although my mother hasn't come, she's been praying for me. I know her. She knows there's nothing she can do for me but pray. I did promise her that I would call every day to let her know I'm okay. The calls stopped, but I try to send an email each day. The days have run together so I'm not sure when the last email was sent. I'm not even sure how long I've been here——weeks, days? The voicemail on my cell phone is full. It hurts too much to listen to the messages.

My sister doesn't come by anymore, either, although I have talked to her on the phone, I think. Or was that an email? She does not feel sorry for me, and I know she is not coming to save me this time. She told me so the last time we had contact. "I don't feel sorry for you, and I won't come save you," she said, "but if you choose 'life,' call me and I'll be there."

I have a niece; she must be almost seven months old now. I wonder what her face looks like. I bet she smells of life, innocence, happiness, and freedom. I wish I were innocent. I was not there when she was born. I was isolated in another place away from her world. The only place I have ever really known, and really hate. I hate that this place of isolation has become more comfortable than failing as the person I want to be. I treat loneliness with isolation; I am sick. I wanted to be a good uncle, a great uncle. I always had the best of intentions and always wanted to be there for my family and my ex-wife. She let me go; she knew I was sick.

About a week ago I tied a belt around a vertical pipe that runs from the floor to the ceiling along the west wall. I know people in jail use belts to hang themselves. I look at it again, knowing I'm probably too weak to reach the pipe overhead to use the video cables.

Stop, just stop. My head will not stop playing the images of the man I never was and have always wanted to be.

That man is too far now—unreachable. I want to die. The prayers of getting robbed and shot on the way to the liquor store didn't work. Sleeping under the bridge to attract a would-be killer didn't work. The prayers of getting cancer so I can die with some dignity didn't work. Alcohol isn't working now, either, causing my entire body to wretch in convulsion as it touches my lips. My mouth tastes like metal, cold iron.

War Games; my mind is eating itself again. Global thermal nuclear war or checkers—life with or without someone to love—regardless, it's still got "me" in it, and there's no way to win at this game. I just want it to stop––the regret, the guilt, the loneliness—me. I wish my head would stop spinning with thoughts and images folding in on themselves. Booze, work, relationships, anything used to stop the hamster wheel from spinning. Now what? I have two choices, kill myself or try life again. Killing me would be easy, I hope. Living is hard, I know.

I hear my mother, "The greatest gift a child can give is that their parents they outlive." Does my phone still work? I tried using it a few days ago to order some food, but I couldn't dial; my brain refused to stop eating itself long enough to put the numbers in the right sequence. I want to die. I'm so tired. I'm just…tired. My mother…God, what I've put her through.

Speed dial, my sister is number one on speed dial; she's a few miles away. I hit the number one on my cell phone, she answers, and I say, "I'm at that point. I can't do it anymore. Come get me."

I chose life.

My sister helps carry my eight-hundred-pound soul out of the loft. She sits next to me through the early morning as I lay in her stepson's bed. I tell her I don't love myself. She tells me she does. That she can love me enough until I can love myself. She sits with her hand on my forehead; I feel a hundred pounds lift. The night terrors start, and I can't sleep, so I concentrate on the toddler clothes hanging in the closet. I notice the little hangers holding little clothes that keep little bodies warm. The bedroom smells of children—life, innocence, happiness, and freedom. God, what I wouldn't give to be that innocent again.

I'm scared, but I chose life. My soul weighs seven hundred pounds.

Part I: The Problem

You *are* the problem…

Chapter 1

Five Reasons You're Not Happy

In its simplest form, you're not happy because you seek happiness outside yourself. Granted, this is no groundbreaking revelation, yet as we look closer at this concept it's revealed why we continually seek externally for happiness. The alternative—looking within ourselves—is difficult, daunting, and scary. Naturally we seek the illusion of an easier way. Consequently, we avoid what feels uncomfortable and difficult until we are forced, usually out of severe emotional pain, to try something different.

Here are five reasons you're not happy:

- ❇ External gratification
- ❇ Lack of meaningful relationships
- ❇ Negative thinking
- ❇ Lack of gratitude
- ❇ Complexity

3

Keep in mind as you read this section that all of these will begin to dissolve away on their own as you move through the seven steps later in this book.

■ External Gratification

Regardless of how much you acquire materially, you will always want more, as it's impossible to have everything. Buddhist monk and author Venerable Henepola Gunaratana explains this paradox well in his book *Mindfulness in Plain English*:

> You can't ever get everything you want. It is impossible. Luckily, there is another option. You can learn to control your mind, to step outside of this endless cycle of desire and aversion. You can learn to not want what you want, to recognize desires but not be controlled by them. This does not mean that you lie down on the road and invite everybody to walk all over you. It means that you continue to live a very normal-looking life but live from a whole new viewpoint. You do the things that a person must do, but you are free from that obsessive, compulsive drivenness of your own desires. You want something, but you don't need to chase after it. You fear something, but you don't need to stand there quaking in your boots. This sort of mental culture is very difficult. It takes years. But trying to control everything is impossible, and the difficult is preferable to the impossible.

Surely you can accept the logic that it's impossible to have everything you want—including control. True happiness and freedom from unsatisfied desires can only be found within self. Finding happiness internally can be uncomfortable but not impossible, **whereas satisfying every desire and expectation is absolutely impossible**. This is why I love the last sentence in the previous excerpt, "The difficult is preferable to the impossible."

■ Lack of Meaningful Relationships

When looking back over my younger years and my struggle to find happiness, it's easy to see now that I was consumed by fear. Fear of not being accepted and loved for who I was completely, even though I realize now I had no idea who I was! Sure, I knew my mother loved me unconditionally and that I was blessed with an amazing childhood, so I don't believe it was due to neglectful parents or some traumatic childhood experience. When and where I developed this fear is not important, rather it's something all of us—at some point in our lives—fear whether we admit it or not. Moreover, how we project ourselves externally—having our sh#$ together—is not always a reflection of how we feel about self.

I confused what I was showing the world on the outside with what I felt on the inside. This is important to note because what the ego portrays externally often hoodwinks us into thinking we have a high self-esteem or feel good about self. It took years of self-examination and work for me to realize this about myself. Honestly, it was something I struggled with deeply as I began my journey towards happiness and living a purposeful life.

After working through the process I describe in this book—and continue to see more clearly in contrast to how I live today—it became painfully obvious that I did not hold self in the highest regard. In hindsight it became evident by the way I had treated myself both physically and emotionally.

The first meaningful relationship you must nurture and prioritize is with self. You must learn to love and accept the consequences of being yourself. Understanding, love, and empathy for self are the seeds from which meaningful relationships grow. Nourished in the soil of love, these relationships blossom into the beautiful flowers that fill the meadows of our life. Love is essential in living a happy life.

In one of the most comprehensive longitudinal studies in history, known as the Grant Study, Harvard researchers examined and followed two hundred sixty-eight men over a period of seventy-two years. The article "What Makes Us Happy?" published in the June 2009 edition of *The Atlantic Magazine*, revealed some amazing insights about happiness. Of all the data collected and examined, the article ascertains the key to happiness is love.

> *Happiness is…"The job isn't conforming; it isn't keeping up with the Joneses. It is playing, and working, and loving. Loving is probably the most important. Happiness is love, full stop."*
> *——George Vaillant, director, the Grant Study*

Before we can develop long lasting, meaningful, and completely fulfilling relationships, we must know how to be open to love, to feel, accept, and give it unconditionally. All of which begins with knowing and loving self.

■ Negative Thinking

Think, and so shall you be. The power of the mind is unquestionable, both in healing and self-defeating aspects of our lives. There is no shortage of self-help and personal development gurus pushing the concept of positive thinking, and we know it works! Yet knowing how life changing positive thinking can be and using it to change your life are two entirely different things. The key to squashing negative thinking is composed of two steps: awareness and practice.

❋ **Awareness**—Do you know what the committee is meeting on today? The committee is the debating society in your head that insists on debating your worthiness as you go about your daily life. Maybe you've heard it before, maybe it's talking to you right now: saying something like, "This guy says some cool stuff…sure he does, but you know you're really too lazy to actually implement any of it… Let's face it, you don't *really* want to be happy. This is as good as it gets, so get used to it!"

The first step in squashing negative thinking is awareness. Even I still talk down to myself at times—often out loud. Shortly after meeting my wife, Emily, I must have verbalized a thought I was having, something like, "That was stupid, you idiot."

7

Her response was simple yet profound, "Hey, don't talk to my friend that way!" Now that *really* made sense to me! We need to be just as supportive of ourselves and our thinking as we would be with a dear friend. Start becoming more aware of your inner dialog.

❋ **Practice**—It took years to develop negative thinking, so changing it naturally takes time. The process of negative thinking began for most in early childhood. The *why* is not important (i.e., society, parents, social influences, etc.). The point is that it developed over time. We weren't born that way. I doubt we came out of the womb thinking, "Great! Bright lights, no more lying around taking it easy, and why is this scary dude spanking me already... surely I've done something wrong." Just as it has taken years to develop negative thinking, so too shall it take time to develop positive thinking. But don't be discouraged. It doesn't take as long as you think! At least not as long as the committee is suggesting right now.

Overcoming negative thinking can be done.

■ Lack of Gratitude

Gratitude is an action. We take care of things we're grateful for. Just as you put oil in your car or maintain other physical possessions you hold dear, you must learn to take care of yourself; this includes body, mind, and spirit. Lack of gratitude fosters feelings of scarcity while increased gratitude creates feelings of abundance. It's simple, really; just think about it for a minute...the last time you experienced deep gratitude will coincide with the feeling that you had everything you needed in that moment if not all aspects of your life. You felt happy.

> *"Gratefulness is the key to a happy life*
> *that we hold in our hands,*
> *because if we are not grateful,*
> *then no matter how much we have*
> *we will not be happy—*
> *because we will always want to have something*
> *else or something more."*
> — *David Steindl-Rast*

■ Complexity

Try making yourself happy... How is that working for you? Happiness is like any other emotion that becomes more elusive as you desperately chase after it. Sometimes the best thing we can do is simplify.

You can't think your way into good living;
you must live your way into good thinking.

It's a simple law of the universe: the more you resist something the more power you give it. Stop chasing after the things society suggests will make you happy. Stop resisting your true authentic self. Later (in step three) we'll be working through acceptance. Acceptance is an important ingredient in the recipe of creating a happy life. The reason acceptance is mentioned with the topic of complexity is that we often become consumed with all the theories or ideas of what happiness is. Accept that true happiness is your birthright; it's already inside you and waiting to be discovered. Stop complicating things with external influences and temporary gratification. Start concentrating on the simple concept of changing the way you live. Live a life in line with the highest ideals and values you have for yourself, and happiness will be the result.

> *"But what is happiness except the simple harmony*
> *between a man and the life he leads?"*
>
> — *Albert Camus*

To know what your values and highest ideals for self are (your authentic self), you must truly know self. You have to live with you 24/7 365; you might as well learn how to be friends. How well do you really know you?

Looking back at the five reasons why you're not happy—external gratification, lack of meaningful relationships, negative thinking, lack of gratitude, and complexity—they may seem a bit overwhelming. Maybe you can identify with some or all of those listed? Regardless, as we work through the process outlined in the rest of this book and you begin to discover your authentic self, these obstacles can and will be turned into assets.

* External gratification—You will find happiness internally by discovering and living true to self.

* Lack of meaningful relationships—Self-love and respect will attract meaningful and loving relationships with others.

* Negative thinking––You will begin to realize how unique, special, and adequate you are just being yourself.

* Lack of gratitude––You will find gratitude for all things, for they have made you who you are.

* Complexity––You will learn to simplify what happiness means and find its abundance in all aspects of life.

Just remember, "The difficult is preferable to the impossible."

Part II: The Solution

Being labeled "the problem" is quite empowering, for you now have access to the solution.

Chapter 2

The Three Keys to Happiness

The biggest secret—which is not really a secret at all—is that life is not a search for happiness. Happiness is a by-product of living a life consistent with the highest ideals and values you have for yourself. Inside all of us lives an ideal, authentic self whom we've hoped or been told we could be. You may not realize it at this moment, but it's in there. Maybe it seems unattainable or obscured by materialistic obsessions, but deep down that ideal self is something we've fallen short of. Maybe we'll get to it someday.

Most people *really* do want to be happy; they just have no idea how to get there. Let me rephrase that… When presented with suggestions like you'll find in this book, most will run away, dismiss it, or put it off because it takes hard work. It's a lot easier to purchase a new 1080i LCD flat screen TV or blame someone else for our unhappiness than work towards humility and building character. Who wants to do that? That is precisely why most people do not work at it, at least not until something painful forces them to do so. Pain is a great motivator.

The First Key to Happiness is: Do something good—from a place of pure unconditional love—in this moment, and the chances that your next moment will be one of happiness greatly increases. It's just that simple.

To experience continued inner-peace and happiness, rinse and repeat.

"Happiness cannot be traveled to, owned, earned, worn, or consumed. Happiness is the spiritual experience of living every minute with love, grace, and gratitude."

—Denis Waitley

Before we can get to this place of living each moment with love, grace, and gratitude, we must get rid of all the trash that's blocking our access to unconditional love, not just of others but, most importantly, of ourselves. Trash is anything that is blocking us from the truth, love, the sunlight of the spirit, God, the universe, or anything we *think* is conspiring against us. To accomplish this, we need to rid ourselves of preconceived notions of what happiness means and how to achieve it.

No matter how you slice it, dice it, word it, explain it, contemplate it, reverse-engineer it, or whatever buzzword we're using to describe happiness today, it all comes down to one simple concept: **being okay with yourself**.

The result of which is an inner-peace and calmness that becomes unshakable over time and with practice.

Inner-peace and happiness go hand in hand. If you're conflicted and fighting within yourself, the world will always appear to be conspiring against you. To put it bluntly, you're just not that important. Once you surrender from this internal battle, you will realize things happen in life around you, not *to* you. One of the most amazing outcomes of working through the seven steps presented in this book and finding happiness is the power of humility.

> *"Humility is not thinking less of yourself but thinking of yourself less."*
>
> —*C.S. Lewis*

The Second Key to Happiness is: Finding love, purpose, and gratitude in each and every moment possible.

The most important aspect of this key is the idea of love. Love and acceptance of our authentic selves are the seeds from which everything else grows. Remember this as we dig deeper into the topic of self-love and emotional connectedness with self throughout the rest of this book.

Many of us know what happiness feels like. We experience glimpses of it during moments of clarity or inner-peace as we become aware of our exact presence in that moment and how significant and perfect it is. Whether gut-busting laughter with friends or enjoying a sunset with a loved one and wishing the moment could last forever, we feel happy. Yet the moment fades, and we're left with trying to recreate it. Like an addict chasing after that first high, we can never quite duplicate it no matter how tirelessly we try.

It's important to realize that most of these brief moments of happiness are when we're outside of ourselves. We're in the company of others or not thinking about our stint in life or personal problems. If alone, we seem to let our worries slip away for a brief moment. Yet, inevitably, past regrets or future fears creep back, sucking us out of the moment like an emotional black hole and robbing us of inner-peace.

Imagine if you could experience that happiness for longer than a fleeting moment!

The Third Key to Happiness is: Maintenance.

I know, maintenance sounds so time consuming and boring, doesn't it? Here's a question: how good are you at scheduled maintenance on your vehicle or equipment you depend on in your daily life?

We take care of things we're grateful for. There was a period in my life that I refer to as my "five-dollar life." I was too busy changing the world and never had time to put more than five dollars' worth of gas in my car—five dollars would actually get you somewhere back then. I know, you'd think it would make more sense to fill up—I had the money, just not the time. Or so I thought. I also never made my bed. What's the point if I'm just going to be messing it up again? My entire life was a mess as I rarely took time to care for the things I owned. It was a real reflection of the way I felt inside.

Do you take care of yourself (i.e., exercise, pray, meditate, eat healthy, etc.)? It's just as important to maintain your spiritual and emotional condition as it is to put oil in your car. If you're not taking care of yourself, then you're not grateful for what you have inside. That needs to change!

You need to discover the good things—assets—inside that you're grateful for and want to take care of. They *are* there; they've just been covered up by external crap and trash that's kept them hidden. In order to uncover them, you need to look at everything and take a complete inventory of yourself.

I know what you're thinking… What if I don't like what I find inside? What if I discover my true authentic self and he/she is a bore or terrible person? I understand. I had the same fears. Fears like, "What if I commit to building character, self-enlightenment, spirituality, living true to self, and find my life is still boring and depressing?" It's like having that secret dream of becoming a singer, dancer, or fireman yet never wholeheartedly attempting to move towards it for fear of failure. It's easier and less disappointing to keep it as a dream. Maybe your fear is like mine, "What if I do achieve my ideal self and I'm still miserable?" Then I'm really screwed. Hope often seems more secure than trying and failing.

If you're afraid of what you'll find inside yourself, that's okay. I, too, was afraid. Yet stepping out into the unknown, trying something completely new and uncomfortable finally became less scary than living my life content with mediocrity. I was desperate, but you don't have to be. All that is required is a little dedication and open-mindedness. However, I must warn you that although the process and steps are simple, they *will* make you uncomfortable. I suggest if you intend to just skim through the rest of this book and not put any of the steps into action, you set the book down and return someday when you're ready for real change.

…Still here?

Awesome, awesome, awesome!

Chapter 3

Feelings About Self Should Come From Self

Have you ever tried to purchase a gift for a friend or loved one you don't know very well? You want to give them something that will bring them happiness, yet you're not quite sure what that is. Or they haven't learned how to create a wish list yet on Amazon.com. So basically you're just taking a shot in the dark. Now take that concept and apply it to yourself. How well do you really know what you need to be happy?

It's hard to be happy when you have no idea what that truly means. Of course you think you know, but why then are you still seeking? At the basic level, all of us really need the same thing: love. However, in order to know what *you* need and how to get it, you must first discover who you are. Then you can plot a path from who you *think* you are now (A) to who you're meant to be (B).

The reason we continue to look for happiness outside ourselves is because the alternative is difficult and scary. Who wants to embark on the laborious journey of self-searching and examination? Especially if that means finding something we don't like about ourselves. God forbid we have to learn to accept it. Acceptance is crucial yet is one of the hardest parts of self-examination; once we accept something, we're responsible. And if we're responsible, we are the ones to blame for our unhappy life.

I don't know about you, but for the majority of my life I had no idea what I needed to be happy. There was always this nagging feeling that someday I would figure it out. In the meantime, I figured if I just kept my nose to the grindstone and charged ahead, I'd eventually find it. I guess, in a sense, that day finally came, but it was a painful lesson in finding inner-peace and happiness. Experience is that way—a painful teacher.

Through self-discovery, I learned something important about myself. I want to be liked—a real shocker. In an attempt to be liked, I sometimes feel responsible for other people's feelings. I guess my thinking was/is that if I protect the feelings of others, I'm a good person; thus they'll like me. If people like me, then I can like myself. The reality is **I cannot alter the lens of others in an attempt to manipulate the way they view me as a person**. This is still looking outside me for happiness.

How others view you is not as important as how you view yourself. Having a realistic view of self is vital to finding what you need to be happy. The main point here is that you are not responsible for how others view you––to some extent. Obviously, if your actions are unacceptable, you're somewhat responsible. Conversely, if you conduct yourself with respect and love for others, you're more likely to receive these same blessings in return. The benefit of the latter is the genuine aspect of it; you're not manipulating someone else's feeling towards you by lying or manipulating the truth about yourself.

In the summer of 2006 (while working through the process I outline in this book), I had a breakthrough. As the result of a simple conversation with a friend, I realized how much of my life I'd been inflating my own self-image by guarding and manipulating the feelings of others—or at least thinking I was. After meeting with a group of friends, one individual asked me specifically if I wanted to join her for a movie. As I'd done a million times before in my life, I made up some lie so as to not hurt her feelings since all I really wanted to do was return home and relax by myself. Here's how it went:

Friend: Hey, do you want to go see a movie?

My mind: *Crap, how do I get out of this…? I know! I just went to the grocery store and need to get some things I have in my car to the fridge.*

Me: (responding almost immediately): Ah, man, I just went to the store and have some ice cream in the car I need to get home.

Friend: Really? What kind?

My mind: *Crap, I need a quick second to come up with something…a flavor of ice cream…stall, stall*

Me: Huh?

Friend: What kind of ice cream?
Me: Rocky Road

I then left and headed home. On the way home I intended to stop by the grocery store to pick up some Rocky Road to settle my conscience. It was then I had an epiphany. Every conversation I had ever had with people where I lied because I didn't want to hurt their feelings flashed through my mind. *Man, I'm sick*, I thought. I called up my life coach and shared my newfound introspection. He then officially gave me permission to use the word "no" without feeling guilt. Moreover, that I could say no without giving excuses and that I am not responsible for other people's feelings. I know it sounds funny, but actually hearing someone giving me permission to say no was exactly what I needed.

Now, obviously, you must not confuse this reasoning with not caring and intentionally hurting someone; that is not what I'm talking about here. I'm talking about feelings about you—more precisely, the feelings you get towards self from others.

The goal is to get the feelings about self from self. When you have an internal deficiency of positive, loving, and healthy feelings towards self, you need to make up for that somewhere, so you look externally. These external forces only add a temporary positive deposit and need to be continually maintained to remain balanced. It becomes a constant struggle to stay balanced, and, honestly, it's freaking exhausting!

What other people think about you is none of your business; what you think of yourself is.

"No one can make you feel inferior
without your consent."

—*Eleanor Roosevelt*

Today I officially give you permission to say no! Try it out… The next time someone asks you to do something you'd rather not do, just say no. That's it. Shut up after that. You're not responsible for the reasons they create in their head. You might be surprised at how few people actually ask you why.

■ We're judged by our actions rather than our intentions.

As I worked through the process in this book, I discovered more than a few amazing things about myself, some of which were hard to accept. Two specific things were: 1) I didn't like who I was, and 2) I lacked a realistic view of myself.

Both of these were difficult to accept since I always viewed myself as having a high self-esteem—yet it was obvious by the way I had been living and treating myself that I wasn't my own best friend. I wasn't very kind to me.

The second discovery was how I presented myself on the outside was not what I was feeling on the inside. It also became apparent that, although I wasn't a bad or mean person, I wasn't as loving and caring to others as I perceived myself to be. My actions weren't always a direct reflection of my intentions. Let's just say my follow-through sucked. The point is, I had an unrealistic view of my relationship with others since it was based on my intentions: what I thought about doing and knew was kind and thoughtful. Yet outwardly I often portrayed something else altogether.

This talk about actions versus intentions may be a little confusing, which I understand. As you work through the process of self-discovery and getting to know your true self through acceptance and self-love, your perception of how you see yourself will change. So, too, will the way you act and behave as your intentions and actions become more in line with each other.

The goal is establishing a healthy and realistic view of self—rather than one based on intentions alone. In our quest for happiness and acceptance, our actions often reflect what we want others to see rather than how we see ourselves. As we begin to know and accept our true self, void of self-serving ego, what we need to be happy becomes more clear and available regardless of how we believe to be perceived by others. As a result, our actions automatically become more altruistic in nature as we need less externally to make us happy. In short, the less we need externally to make us happy, the more pure and good our intentions and motives become.

Again, happiness is the result of living a life true to one's ideal self and values. Wow, that sounds easy right? The reason why people struggle with this concept is they have no idea what their ideal self looks like. More than likely, they're striving towards an ideal self they feel expected to have or were given and that feels like a pair of shoes a size too small. Moreover, those who have an ideal self in mind often feel it's unattainable. Worse yet, and most terrifying of all, was the fear I had and described earlier: **what if I strive for this "ideal" self, achieve it, and I'm still miserable?** Then what?

The answer to that question can be summed up in one simple statement:

> *"If you want something you have never had,*
> *you must do something you've never done."*

>   *—Author Unknown*

The only question left is: What are you willing to do to discover your ideal authentic self and find happiness?

■ Your First Action Assignment

Before you read any further in this book, I want you to take a moment and write down what your ideal self looks like. Included in appendix (a) is the **Ideal Self Worksheet** to help you with the process. Don't worry if you find it difficult or vague. This is just a baseline for you to start from. Your true authentic self will reveal itself as you work through the seven steps in Part III.

Chapter 4

Taking Out The Trash

*"Happiness is when what you think, what you say,
and what you do are in harmony."*

——Ghandi

I believe Gandhi's view of happiness to be right on. Thus, we need to get three things in harmony: our thoughts, words, and actions. The result of such harmony is a healthy self-image based in reality. Happiness is the by-product of having our thoughts, words, and actions in harmony with our authentic self.

It has been my experience that thoughts, words, and actions based upon love bring the greatest serenity and happiness into our lives. This begins with love for self as it extends outward. Personally, I did not wake up one day and love everything and everyone. How could I? I did not truly love myself—or so I discovered through this process.

It has been a long journey and one that continues on a day-to-day basis.

When looking at these three areas, there appears to be a paradox. You have to do (action) and say (words) the right things in order to think (thought) healthy about yourself and your world in order to be happy (i.e., you can't think your way into good living; you must live your way into good thinking). It's all about action. **You cannot intellectualize and read about happiness and wake up one day happy**. It just doesn't work that way, at least not for me or anyone else I've known. Yet in order to do the right things (action), you have to think them first. That is why it is important to realize this journey is a process. It takes practice and gets easier over time. Eventually, the right thoughts are the first to come into your mind, followed by the right actions, the natural result being self-respect and a positive self-image based in reality.

I must point out why I use the phrase *based in reality*. As we discussed briefly earlier, it's easy to confuse actions with intentions. Our intention doesn't mean squat if not followed with appropriate action, which can lead to a skewed perception of how we are actually perceived by others.

In short, your head is full of crap. Whether you realize it or not, there are thousands of thoughts running through your head every millisecond; most of them are sabotaging your ability to be happy. The result of working through the following seven steps is simple yet not easy. Take inventory of your thoughts, character traits, fears, etc.—the good and the bad—keep the good and discover what you can learn from the perceived bad, and then let it go. It's about accepting who you are completely, embracing humility, and realizing that the power to be completely happy is already inside of you waiting to be unleashed. Happiness is your natural, authentic state.

Here are the steps we're going to take together:

Step 1 — Awareness

Step 2 — Surrender

Step 3 — Acceptance

Step 4 — Self-Searching and Inventory Management

Step 5 — Atonement and Forgiveness

Step 6 — Spirituality

Step 7 — Maintenance

I hope you took the time to fill out the Ideal Self Worksheet found in appendix a. I encourage you to be completely honest with yourself and just write down whatever comes to your mind. Write down what you strive to achieve in yourself or habits, vices, or character traits you wish you could change or wish you had. Again, this is only a baseline to see where you're at and help you start to visualize where you want to go.

Before we get into the steps directly, I'd like to make something clear on the topic of spirituality. All that is required is that you believe in the possibility that there may be something outside of self, outside of your control, which (whether you believe it to be real or not) can, may, or will provide you with some type of guidance in your life.

Call it God, Buddha, the Universe, a Greater Conscience, etc., it doesn't matter. If you believe you are the center of the universe, this isn't going to work. If you're not sure, go outside and look up. Do you know what's out there, beyond what your eyes can see or mind can comprehend?

Let's get started.

Part III: Seven Steps to Discovering and Loving Your Authentic Self

"The image of myself which I try to create in my own mind in order that I may love myself is very different from the image which I try to create in the minds of others in order that they may love me."

—W.H. Auden

Chapter 5

Awareness

"Awareness is empowering."

—*Rita Wilson*

I've always liked the saying, "I didn't know what I didn't know." For years I was unaware there existed a better way to live, a life based on the acceptance and knowing of my authentic self that could bring true inner-peace and happiness. Character building, in terms of living a purposeful and fulfilling life, was not something I sought for happiness but rather as a means to obtain something, a tool rather than a virtue.

At age twenty-two, I fulfilled a childhood dream by becoming a full-time zookeeper—primate keeper. I was happy...for a few years. Then one day I woke up and realized I wasn't happy anymore. It was that moment when I discovered a deep awareness that no matter what I accomplished in life, I would never be satisfied. I felt it in my soul.

For the next sixteen years, I continued to search for satisfaction outside of myself. With each new job or relationship, I was fulfilled for a while, but eventually the dissatisfaction with life would return. Although I was aware of this uneasy and restless feeling, I had no idea what it was, what to do about it, or that there was even a solution.

Not until I was forced out of pain and desperation to seek a different way of living did I become aware of the source of my unhappiness and dissatisfaction with life. I was trying to fill an internal hole with material (external) things. Out of this awareness came the greatest discovery of all: I could not fix myself.

■ Awareness

The first step to inner-peace and happiness is awareness. This awareness is composed of two parts: 1) the awareness that something needs to change and 2) awareness of your thoughts and inner dialog.

In regards to change, I'm talking about real change here, not geographical, professional, or material, but a significant change in your perception of the world and your place in it.

Change of this magnitude must come from outside self. Yes, I know this point is counterintuitive to what most think of the term *self-help*. My journey consisted of finding those who had what I wanted—true inner-peace, happiness, and serenity—and asking them for help and taking action on the suggestions they provided. Even though the decision to make a change came from within self, the actions that followed required guidance and help from forces outside myself.

This idea that change must come from outside self may be difficult to grasp at first; after all, haven't we always heard that real change must start from within? To some extent this is true, but be honest with yourself, if you have the capacity to make this change, why haven't you done so? The awareness is the realization that you need help and a new perspective, something you cannot get on your own.

> *"We can't solve problems by using the same kind of thinking we used when we created them."*
>
> ——Albert Einstein

■ Meditation and Thought Awareness

To discover just how self-sabotaging your thoughts can be, you need awareness of what your thoughts are telling you about yourself. One such way is through the power of meditation. One myth is that meditation is all about thinking nothing or clearing the mind. There are different types of meditation; one such type is Vipassana, which means having insight or acute awareness of what is happening as it is happening. This type of meditation helps us become aware of our thoughts as we're thinking them.

Whether or not you've tried Vipassana meditation, you should seriously consider it. If you're interested in a simple guide, I highly suggest an awesome book titled *Mindfulness in Plain English* by Venerable Henepola Gunaratana. Gunaratana explains that meditation is not easy yet is invaluable in harnessing the power of awareness. The following section from this amazing book expresses the importance of becoming aware of our thoughts and feelings. The section I chose from the book below is a bit lengthy. I tried several times to shorten the excerpt but felt it was all too valuable. The emotions and concept describe me perfectly. I'm sure you'll find some familiar emotions in this section as I did.

Meditation is not easy. It takes time and it takes energy. It also takes grit, determination, and discipline. It requires a host of personal qualities which we normally regard as unpleasant and which we like to avoid whenever possible. We can sum it all up in the American word "gumption." Meditation takes "gumption." It is certainly a great deal easier just to kick back and watch television. So why bother? Why waste all that time and energy when you could be out enjoying yourself? Why bother? Simple. Because you are human. And just because of the simple fact that you are human, you find yourself heir to an inherent unsatisfactoriness in life which simply will not go away. You can suppress it from your awareness for a time. You can distract yourself for hours on end, but it always comes back—usually when you least expect it. All of a sudden, seemingly out of the blue, you sit up, take stock, and realize your actual situation in life.

There you are, and you suddenly realize that you are spending your whole life just barely getting by. You keep up a good front.

You manage to make ends meet somehow and look okay from the outside. But those periods of desperation, those times when you feel everything caving in on you, you keep those to yourself. You are a mess. And you know it. But you hide it beautifully. Meanwhile, way down under all that you just know there has got be some other way to live, some better way to look at the world, some way to touch life more fully. You click into it by chance now and then. You get a good job. You fall in love. You win the game, and for a while, things are different. Life takes on a richness and clarity that makes all the bad times and humdrum fade away. The whole texture of your experience changes and you say to yourself, "Okay, now I've made it; now I will be happy." But then that fades, too, like smoke in the wind. You are left with just a memory. That and a vague awareness that something is wrong.

But there is really another whole realm of depth and sensitivity available in life; somehow, you are just not seeing it. You wind up feeling cut off. You feel insulated from the sweetness of experience by some sort of sensory cotton. You are not really touching life. You are not making it again. And then even that vague awareness fades away, and you are back to the same old reality. The world looks like the usual foul place, which is boring at best. It is an emotional roller coaster, and you spend a lot of your time down at the bottom of the ramp, yearning for the heights.

So what is wrong with you? Are you a freak? No. You are just human. And you suffer from the same malady that infects every human being. It is a monster in side all of us and it has many arms: Chronic tension, lack of genuine compassion for others, including the people closest to you, feelings being blocked up, and emotional deadness. Many, many arms. None of us is entirely free from it. We may deny it. We try to suppress it. We build a whole culture around hiding from it, pretending it is not there, and distracting ourselves from it with goals and projects and status. But it never goes away. It is a constant undercurrent in every thought and every perception; a little wordless voice at the back of the head saying, "Not good enough yet. Got to have more. Got to make it better. Got to be better." It is a monster, a monster that manifests everywhere in subtle forms.

Go to a party. Listen to the laughter, that brittle-tongued voice that says fun on the surface and fear underneath. Feel the tension, feel the pressure. Nobody really relaxes. They are faking it. Go to a ball game. Watch the fan in the stand. Watch the irrational fit of anger. Watch the uncontrolled frustration bubbling forth from people that masquerades under the guise of enthusiasm, or team spirit. Booing, catcalls, and unbridled egotism in the name of team loyalty. Drunkenness, fights in the stands. These are the people trying desperately to release tension from within. These are not people who are at peace with themselves. Watch the news on TV. Listen to the lyrics in popular songs. You find the same theme repeated over and over in variations. Jealousy, suffering, discontent, and stress.

Life seems to be a perpetual struggle, some enormous effort against staggering odds. And what is our solution to all this dissatisfaction? We get stuck in the "If only" syndrome. If only I had more money, then I would be happy. If only I could find somebody who really loves me, if only I could lose twenty pounds, if only I had a color TV, Jacuzzi, and curly hair, and on and on forever. So where does all this junk come from and more important, what can we do about it? It comes from the conditions of our own minds. It is a deep, subtle, and pervasive set of mental habits, a Gordian knot which we have built up bit by bit and we can unravel just the same way, one piece at a time. We can tune up our awareness, dredge up each

separate piece, and bring it out into the light. We can make the
unconscious conscious, slowly, one piece at a time.

Ah, there it was, in the second to last sentence, **"We can tune up our awareness, dredge up each separate piece, and bring it out into the light**." That's important! That is what we're going to do!

You may find it too difficult to meditate at this point in your happiness journey. What you can do is start tuning into the committee (your thoughts) and pay attention to what they're telling you about yourself.

■ Awareness Action: Thought Awareness

Your exercise for this step is fairly simple, at least on paper. If you're not used to being completely aware of what you're thinking, this might be a little more difficult. The exercise is using a thought journal to increase awareness of your inner dialog.

If you're like me, it's difficult at times to stop your mind on one single thought. By writing down what I'm thinking, not worrying about grammar, syntax, or the way it sounds, I get a better understanding and awareness of where I'm at mentally, emotionally, and spiritually. When I first started this practice I carried a Moleskin pocket-sized notebook around in my pocket to jot down my thoughts anytime I had a spare moment.

The power behind this exercise isn't so much what you write in your journal as it is the action of becoming aware of your thoughts. Pay attention to your inner voice and what it's telling you. Become aware of how you perceive yourself and the tone of your inner dialog. The first step in changing this dialog is awareness.

Get yourself a notebook or journal. Better yet, get several. Keep one by your bed, in your car, in your desk, and start jotting down your thoughts, feelings, and emotions. Again, it's not how you write. Just put down on paper whatever it is you're feeling and thinking as often as you can. Continue your thought journal, and within a few weeks you'll begin to notice how you're treating yourself mentally.

Chapter 6

Surrender

When you surrender, it generally helps to let the other side know.

Surrender is about letting go. It's a control thing. By concentrating on wants and desires (which are never satisfied), you miss out on what you need. What you need to be happy and spiritually fit comes from within and can be found in the moment you're in right now, not the moments you're dreaming of in the future.

> *"You must give up the life you planned in order to have the life that is waiting for you."*
>
> —Joseph Campbell

To surrender is to yield or give up control. Surrendering can be difficult as it deals with two areas we often struggle with: faith and control.

■ Faith

When living in the moment, little faith is needed. This moment is exactly what it is, no expectations, just is. Experience it, allow it to be, allow it to teach.

A definition of faith from Webster's:
1) firm belief in something for which there is no proof

You certainly have no proof of anything in the future. What you do have is experience; experience that if you help someone else, as opposed to doing something selfish, you'll feel better about self. You then know from experience that when you do the best you can, the outcome is more acceptable, whatever it may be. By doing the best you can in each moment, you're less invested emotionally in the outcome as you develop the faith that everything will work out.

So you do have faith. Faith that if you take the right action in this moment, something you have no proof of— the future—will work out the way its supposed to.

Faith in this context is not associated with the spiritual realm or religion; it's about developing faith in oneself and your ability to handle whatever life throws at you. This type of faith is created in each moment by doing what we know is right and loving towards self and others— assuming you know what that is. Don't fret, little camper, if you're asking, "What if I don't know what is right and loving towards self and others?" That's certainly a good question and one that becomes clearer as you begin to discover your authentic self. In its simplest form, the answer is revealed in our motives: is it based in love or preservation of self-serving ego?

Faith doesn't normally appear out of nowhere. I did not wake up one morning, reach in my nightstand, and pull out faith. There was no shining moment with clouds parting that launched me towards a faithful existence. Faith started with a series of events, thoughts, and a realization. The series of events consisted of failed relationships, the passing of a friend, a lost job, and utter defeat. Everything had led me to this intersection in my life, a moment of clarity when the universe handed me the most precious gift of all—desperation. I reached the point where the emotional pain and fear of where my life was heading outweighed the fear of trying something completely different. I had to let go of *everything*, every idea of what I thought my life was about, from the meaning of success to how I viewed the world and my place in it. **It was the realization that my ego was a black hole constantly pulling me away from my authentic self**. A black hole—never satisfied—and consuming everything in its path. I realized it was time to stop resisting. I took a leap of faith that somehow, someway, I just might come out on the other side. For me—at that point—surrender was easy. I really had no other choice as the alternative was giving up on life altogether.

"Suicide is a permanent solution to a temporary problem."

—*Phil Donahue*

The reason most people never reach the point of complete surrender—the release of their ego—is that they simply aren't in enough pain. The amazing thing about surrender and finding true happiness is you can choose to avoid most of the pain. However, you must convince the ego that control is only an illusion.

Lack of faith comes from lack of experience. Lack of experience in this context comes from the continuous struggle to maintain control. You think you surrender something and let it go by acting like you don't care; yet, if you look closely, you're still emotionally attached to the outcome.

■ Get Over It

Of course there are those of us who lack faith because—in our minds—everything bad happens to us. Again, this is the ego talking, making us feel as if the entire universe is conspiring against us. That's ludicrous. Things happen in life around us, not to us. Again, to put it bluntly, we're just not *that* important. And yes, certainly there are those who intentionally hurt others, but this isn't about them, it's about changing you! It's time to get over it.

The realization has to be yours that at some point you are responsible for your own happiness. Constantly blaming circumstances for your misfortune will only keep you in the position of the victim. Victims are spectators in their own lives. You are a survivor; survivors take charge and let events, no matter how tragic, take them to where they're supposed to be. And you, my friend, are supposed to be happy! Happiness *is* your birthright—start claiming it!

■ Self-Fulfilling Prophecy

> *"Whether you think that you can, or that you can't, you are usually right."*

——Henry Ford

The self-fulfilling prophecy——it's a simple concept and logically makes sense when looked at from an objective view. What we fear the most often manifests itself in our lives because we give power and purpose to it by constantly worrying about it. For example, take one of my previous relationships.

I'm unworthy of true unconditional love. Through this belief about self, I enter a relationship with someone, self-destruct or do as many things wrong as possible—— mostly unaware while blaming others for my misfortune. Eventually the person has had enough and leaves me, thus proving and validating my belief about self that I'm unlovable. That's the short version, but many relationships happen this way; by placing unreasonable demands on ourselves or our partners, we drive them away and validate our own feelings of inadequacy.

This has to do with faith in a different light—the belief or feeling that things will turn out negatively because they always have. In this mindset, we unknowingly have

47

faith based on past experiences and project them as likely outcomes of any future events or experiences. It just makes sense that if we expect a certain outcome, we're more likely to manifest things in our lives that bring them into reality.

Think about people you know whose lives seem to always go their way. Somehow they always seem to land on their feet and succeed at whatever they do. I had a friend like that growing up; it seemed he always succeeded at everything. I remember one certain instance when we were out rabbit hunting and he bet me he could throw a quarter in the air and hit it with his .22 rifle. I was thinking that's impossible... Sure enough, he threw it up and shot it, not once, but three times in a row. He just believed he could, and so he did. Most of my life I believed I couldn't, so I didn't.

Looking back, now I realize the seed was there, the belief that I was great. There was always a nagging of my authentic self telling me I was great, yet I didn't believe it for some reason or another. Today I not only believe it, but I know and experience it. You can and will, too!

"Faith is daring the soul to go beyond what the eyes can see."

—*William Newton Clark*

■ Spiritual Faith

Up to this point we've talked about faith as it relates to personal experience. Faith of that kind is good, but experience alone sometimes is not enough as it's skewed by our fallible perception. A large part of my faith comes from a power outside of me. Call it God, Buddha, Allah, Creator, or whatever—the concept is simple, it's about humility.

Each morning and evening I get on my knees and pray. I pray for guidance in the morning and for others and thanks in the evening. If a day has me facing a stressful situation such as a job interview or something, I find a quiet place and hit my knees and pray for acceptance of whatever the outcome may be.

Surveys conducted by Gallup concluded that those who are spiritually committed described themselves as "very happy" twice as often as people less religious or spiritually committed [1].

My family and I attended church every Sunday until I was five years old and we moved to a farm. Years later when my grandfather died, I remember all of these people saying, "He's in a better place now." I knew what they were referring to but couldn't understand or believe that to be true. Yet at the same time, there was a glimpse of hope or relief that maybe they were right. And most importantly I remember thinking, "Who cares if they're right or wrong, it sure seems to be helping them cope."

> *"The road that is built in hope is more pleasant to the*
> *traveler than the road built in despair, even*
> *though they both lead to the same destination."*

> *—Marian Zimmer Bradley*

Faith is an essential part of happiness. Seek it.

■ Control

The cliché "I have no control over people places and things" sticks in my craw sometimes. It keeps us in the role of the victim. The key to control is, again, staying in the moment, or harnessing the power of now—are you seeing a theme here? *This moment* is where your actions count, the actions that create your future. So you do have some control. You have control over a lot of things actually.

An example: I'm minding my own *moment* while waiting at a red light. In front of me is a man talking on his cell phone. I'm thinking of how dangerous cell phones are while driving when the light changes to green. The gentleman continues his conversation without noticing the light has changed. I feel a little swell of anger. Now I'm *in tune* with this feeling, I'm in the moment and aware of my surroundings. So instead of anger, I switch to gratitude. I'm grateful for having a car and home to drive to…heck, I'm grateful I have two arms to hold this steering wheel! I gently honk my horn, and the man waves and drives forward. I'm happy to be on my way and into the next moment.

I have control over my reaction to situations, which has an impact on my future. Suppose I would have gotten angry, yelled at the guy, and flipped him off. Drove home in a fit of anger and pretty much wasted a good thirty minutes if not the entire evening. Not only did I create more misery, I missed every single moment while consumed with anger. At that point, I have lost control.

When you're in the moment, you're in reality and not creating fear out of some illusion. So, to eliminate fear, stay in the moment.

■ Stop Fighting

The most amazing things happen when you surrender, give up control, and stop fighting. By giving up on the life you dreamed of, you break free of expectation and your limited imagination of what's possible. You begin to realize the possibility of a life beyond that which you're even capable of dreaming.

By surrendering to the idea that you are not the center of the universe, self-serving ego is no longer your master. You become part of something larger and realize it's not all about you as you begin to experience empathy for self and others. In hindsight, the lack of self-love in all those years of living life based in ego and self-preservation will be revealed. If you truly loved and respected self, you wouldn't treat yourself the way you often do. In the constant struggle to gather acceptance and validation from outside sources, you compromise morals, values, and dignity. The amazing gift of self-love and the realization that everything you need to be happy and whole is already within you allows you to lower expectations of self and others. The result is the ability to accept and give love unconditionally.

"Even after all this time the sun never says to the Earth, 'You owe me.' Look what happens with a love like that. It lights up the whole sky."

—Hafiz

Our ego tells us who we should be, how we should live, and the definition of success and happiness, which is a lie because it's all based on external sources. The truth—as Dr. Wayne Dyer suggests—is that everything we need to be happy and fulfilled is already inside of us, given to use by our creator. The same force that gave us everything we needed in the womb is still with us; thus we still have access to anything we need to live our life on purpose. We just need to get our ego out of the way, be open-minded, willing, and let the universe bring it to us. However, we must not confuse this idea with procrastination; we must take action to prepare ourselves in being ready and able to recognize these moments and gifts as they arrive. Anything else is still primarily our ego talking.

If everything we need to become who we are is already within us, why do we continually seek outside of ourselves for happiness and purpose? Because we're still living for and by ego, telling us if only we had this or that we'd be happy.

We all have an inner voice telling us there must be something more, some purpose to our lives. Start listening to it! Think about how you lean in to overhear a conversation that catches your interest. Maybe you're thinking these people are weak or you're too proud to ask them questions, but you still sort of lean in and want to know more. Start listening to that need to know and want more out of life and let it take you to where you're destined to go.

■ Surrender Actions

1. Turning It Over and Letting Go

Surrender is composed of two parts: letting go and turning it over. Following is a practical exercise to illustrate the difference in letting go and turning something over.

Grab an object like a rock (or anything) and hold it tightly in your hand with your palm facing up. With palm still facing upwards, open your hand and let go. What happens?

It's still there.

You may have let it go, but you still haven't turned it over completely; you still desire control over it or are lacking faith in some sense.

Now, repeat the process, but after you've opened your hand, turn your wrist and arm so your palm is facing down. What happens?

The object falls.

Gravity takes over, just as the universe will when you truly turn something over.

The most difficult part is not bending over to pick it back up, it's to have faith it's where it's supposed to be.

I practice this exercise when I'm having a hard time turning something over or surrendering. I usually do this in bed if I can't sleep. I use the thought of what's bothering me in place of the physical object while extending my arms out in front of me. I visualize the problem or issue along with all the alternatives or actions I can take. If I have done everything I believe I can at that moment, I imagine the problem as the object in my hands, let go, and turn it over.

2. What Can You Do About It Right Now?

This is a simple—and obvious to some—exercise a counselor helped me with years ago as I was struggling with certain aspects of my life, feeling overwhelmed with bills, taxes, my living situation, job...pretty much life in general. She had me write down each *issue* I was worried about on a yellow legal pad—one item per line. We went through each item and she asked, "Is there something you can do about this today, right now?" If the answer was yes, we did it. Yes, she helped me... Well, sort of. For example, one issue was—having just lost my job—the uncertainty of how I was going to afford paying the lease on my SUV. My action was to get the appropriate paperwork and phone numbers together, and the next time we met (a few days later) we would call together. Of course she didn't call for me, and I can't remember if she was even in the room when I made the call, but for some reason it helped. It may seem odd that I was stressed about something so simple as making a phone call, but at that time in my life everything was just so overwhelming. The process of breaking things down into digestible little actions made them all more manageable.

This exercise and the action of writing things down helps in many ways:

* First, it's usually a much shorter list on paper than it was in your head!

* Secondly, you can look at each item and determine if there's any action you can take in that exact moment. Maybe it's not the right time of day or you need to get some other things in order first, but if there is something you can do, **do it**! If you need help, ask someone. If not, make a note of what else you need to cross it off the list and either take that action or let it go. It's on paper now; it's not going anywhere.

For your convenience, I've included in appendix (b), a simple worksheet and more practical tips and an amazing exercise for surrendering and letting things go. Check it out.

References:

1.   Religion in America, The Gallup Report No. 222

Chapter 7

Acceptance

As a result of the first two steps, awareness and surrender, you're now becoming aware that you need to change some aspect of your life to find true long-lasting happiness. Yet simply being aware will not accomplish anything if you're unwilling to change that aspect of your life. This is where acceptance comes in. You must be able to accept what it is you need to change. If you can't get to a place of acceptance—recognizing the reality of what is standing in your way—you're stuck. In some cases this can also be referred to as denial.

The unwillingness to change something is based in fear. Fear that without this crutch or *thing* blocking your way, what will define you? One of the biggest reasons we stay stuck in life is because it's comfortable; yes, it sounds absurd, I know. Regardless of how uncomfortable or dissatisfied we are with life, it's what we know, and change is scary. No worries. Just because you accept something doesn't mean you have to change or face the magnitude of it immediately. All that is needed for a start is acceptance and a smidgen of willingness.

There's certainly evidence that, in some cases, denial can be a beneficial coping mechanism, at least in the short term, for example, in dealing with the loss of a loved one. This is something I dealt with after losing my father suddenly in July of 2010.

■ Don't Confuse Acceptance with Liking

Since having worked through the process outlined herein, I had the amazing experience of accepting my father for who he was: a simple, hardworking man who expressed his love in various ways. Prior to my personal journey into finding happiness, it's accurate to say I held some deep-rooted resentment towards my father.

When I was five, my father moved us from our modest home in the city to a dilapidated farmhouse in the middle of nowhere to pursue his dream of farming. He also continued to work as a construction foreman during the day and would farm on nights and weekends. I do have fond memories of being squeezed in next to him on our John Deere tractor—my head banging against the glass as we bumped along—while he demonstrated the artful process of plowing. It was magical the way he would get within a few feet of the fence line, arms and legs maneuvering all sorts of levers, while turning the tractor on a dime and heading the other direction only to repeat the process seamlessly. I also recall the first time he let me attempt this artful process... Let's just say we spent the rest of the weekend pulling fence.

What I remember most of my father when I was a child was he worked a lot. My mother taught me how to throw a baseball and slide into second base, things most would associate having learned from their fathers. He didn't coach any of my baseball teams but did make it to most of my high school basketball games. As the result of self-discovery and my journey into finding happiness, I discovered some resentment towards my father. Mostly that we didn't have the close relationship I dearly wanted or thought I deserved. I began working on self-acceptance first, and out of that came forgiveness and acceptance of my father simply for who he was. Moreover, if I wanted a different relationship with him, it was up to me—I needed to learn his love language.

I began to see my father in a whole different way. Like how he showed his love by providing for his family. Being a provider was his measurement of success as a father, husband, and man. It's all he knew and if I wanted a different relationship it was up to *me* to change. Whether it was me changing or him, I'm not sure, but as he got older he started to soften up a bit and was getting better at expressing his emotions. Starting about a year before he died, he would even call me on the phone every now and then just to see how I was doing. Acceptance, forgiveness, and my inner journey towards happiness were the foundation for the amazing relationship we were developing.

On Friday, June 25, 2010, my mother called and said, "They found five tumors in Dad's brain." I knew this couldn't be good. For some reason—experience, logic, who knows—I had a feeling it was cancer and that with five tumors in his brain, the cancer probably started somewhere else and had metastasized through his body. The next day, a biopsy of a lump on his neck confirmed our fears and my suspicion: terminal lung cancer. **Cue up denial**.

I recalled the surgeon's remark in the little room outside surgery the day they biopsied his lymph node, "It's terminal lung cancer. All we can do is pray God has mercy and he doesn't suffer." As my mother and I rode the elevator with dad after he was out of recovery, he looked up at us from his gurney and asked, "Is it cancer?" We both said "yes." I then looked him right in the eye, held his hand, and said "it is what it is." I'd like to think I told him I loved him in that moment, but I'm not sure. And I wonder if what I did say was cold or somehow less compassionate than I could have been in that moment. But that's making it about me, and it certainly wasn't.

It was tough seeing my father face his mortality so suddenly. Initially I was concerned with helping him come to terms with the situation. But after discussing it with my wife and spiritual advisor, it became clear that my only job was to be a son. That getting right with self and God was his journey and nothing I had control over.

My wife and I had already planned a trip to Florida for a few days to spend some time with a good friend, and we debated on whether or not we should still go. We ended up going, and I talked to my father every day on the phone during our short four-day trip. I remember vividly thinking that although no one had actually discussed how much time he had, I was optimistically thinking six to nine months would be a miracle. This left me with the reality that—years from now—I would look back on this period and wonder if I did everything I should have.

My wife and I returned from our trip on July 4 and traveled home to see my father the next day. We spent a few hours together, talked about work, racing, and the usual stuff for us. He sat in his La-Z-Boy chair, turning his head ever so slightly at times to better position his good ear towards the conversation. I told him I loved him, hugged him, and we left. The next night, July 6, 2010, just after my wife and I had gone to bed, the phone rang. It was my mother. The paramedics could be heard in the background, and she was explaining that Dad had collapsed on the kitchen floor and had stopped breathing. I still remember her telling the paramedics—apparently after they learned he was recently diagnosed with terminal lung cancer—that he wanted to live. My sister and niece were there at the time, and he was later pronounced dead at the hospital. We didn't request an autopsy but since previous CT scans had shown a few blood clots in his legs, best guess was a pulmonary embolism.

I spoke at his funeral. "He was a hard worker," I said, "and he's finally getting the vacation and rest he deserves." Dad was always on time; prompt he was. So I know it was his time to go. As I shared with the hundreds that showed up to his funeral, "I can accept it, but I don't have to like it."

After hearing about my father, a good friend who had recently lost his mother told me, "It may not make much sense now, but death is a tragic thing but it can also be very beautiful." At the time I thought he was crazy. But the amazing thing about this whole process of finding happiness is the ability to have an open mind and be receptive to the beauty in life regardless of how tragic or chaotic it seems.

The day before the funeral, my wife, mother, sister, four-year-old niece, and I were looking through photos to show at the service. My sister had explained to my niece what had happened, and as we were looking through photos she said, "It's too bad Grandpa died, but it's great that we have these pictures of him." That's beautiful, I think. I'm so grateful I have memories of a loving father and a great man. That is something I did; I made a choice to have a better relationship with him, and *acceptance* made it possible.

Again, it's important to note that just because you accept something does not mean you have to like it. This may be difficult to understand, but as we grow spiritually and emotionally, acceptance becomes easier—even if means facing something uncomfortable. For out of experience and practice grows the faith in knowing we are going to grow as a result.

■ News Flash: You're Responsible

The most difficult part of acceptance is... **drum roll, please**... knowing that **once you accept something, you are responsible**. This means you are the only one who can do something about it. If you're like me, that can be a tough pill to swallow and something that keeps you in the victim role—powerless to change—for many years.

"Acceptance is not submission; it is acknowledgment of the facts of a situation. Then deciding what you're going to do about it."

——*Kathleen Casey Theisen*

That's right, you, and no one else. The blame game is over. You can no longer play the victim and blame someone else for your misfortune.

No real change can occur until you reach a point of acceptance. Until then, there is simply no real motivation to do so. From acceptance grows the willingness and possibility of a solution.

■ Moving with the Flow of the Universe

It's a common belief that there's an ebb and flow to the universe. Maybe you believe in Newton's third law of motion: that for every action there is always an equal and opposite reaction. Whatever the reasoning, resistance makes things harder. That's easy to understand. When life throws us something unexpected, our first reaction may be to resist; that's natural. But resisting what *is* just makes things more difficult. Sure, it's easy to say and hard to put into practice, but it gets easier over time and with a little practice.

Recently I've done something that I've always dreamed of doing, competing in a triathlon. As with most newbie triathletes, my swimming needed some improvement. Prior to the triathlon, I had recently completed a half marathon so I figured I was in pretty good shape and thought I was a fairly efficient freestyle swimmer. I soon realized after only a few laps in the pool I was exhausted. So I totally stressed out about the swimming leg of the triathlon and did a majority of my first race in the back and sidestroke.

Being determined—and a little obsessive at times—I went in search of ways to become a better swimmer and came across Terry Laughlin's *Total Immersion Swimming* DVD series. I realized my swimming technique was totally off and I was causing more resistance than necessary. With a little practice I've become a more efficient swimmer and now actually look forward to the swimming leg of triathlons.

With a little practice you can learn to stop resisting whatever life throws your way. Accept the idea that if something is causing you discomfort or it's more difficult than it should be, maybe you're resisting in same way. It *is what it is*, or as my father-in-law says, "A redheaded girl is a redheaded girl." Stop resisting so you can get into the solution.

■ A Note on Self-Acceptance

Although there is a vast amount of information on self-acceptance—and, yes, it's essential to happiness—that is not what we're discussing here. Self-acceptance will begin to manifest within you naturally as a result of working through the entire process outlined in this book. As a result, the acceptance we're discussing here will become more natural and easier as your happiness and emotional health depends less on circumstances outside self.

■ Acceptance Action: Get it on Paper

Make a list of things you're having trouble accepting; put each one on a separate line with plenty of space in between. Don't think about why or if you should put them down, just write them down. (I know it's scary).

Here's one from my past…

Bills. At one point in my life I was not living very responsibly and had a large shoebox full of old bills I hadn't paid or had just neglected to open; terrible, I know. It was full of all sorts of stuff, doctor bills, student loans, credit cards, utility and cable bills, etc. I even moved several times and took the box with me, determined to open them all someday. Needless to say, my credit rating was… well, bad. For some reason I just didn't want to accept the fact that I owed all these people money. And forget about calling them and working something out; how terrifying is that? Well, I'm glad to report that as I began my happiness journey I got some help with that shoebox (starting in late 2006). I asked for help in getting my financial situation organized, and amazingly the creditors were understanding and were eager to work something out with me. I'm happy to say my credit today is pretty good. That shoebox of unopened bills was a reflection of all the things in my life I was afraid to accept and confront.

The fear of the unknown and consequences we create in our minds are almost always worse than reality.

Getting back to your list——below each item, write down what it is you fear. And surely there is a fear there. Fear of being discovered for a fraud, fear of losing someone you love, fear of being broke, fear that there's nothing you can do about it, etc. Whatever it is, there is a reason why you do not want to accept it. Finding what's at the root of the fear will help reveal the answer.

Next, take your list and revisit Surrender Action 2 in Chapter 6: What Can You Do About It Right Now?

Chapter 8

Self-Searching and Inventory Management

Now that we've begun the process of accepting that something needs to change, we can identify what areas we need to work on through self-searching. Remember, just because we accept something does not mean we have to like it.

The purpose of self-searching is like inventory management. When I worked in the restaurant business, every food item had a shelf life. Raw chicken, three days below forty degrees Fahrenheit; chopped broccoli, five days. After the shelf life had expired, we threw it out for it was no longer considered a salable item.

Self-searching is about identifying parts of our thinking, perception, or character traits that are salable and add value to our lives and are part of our authentic self——and those which are hindering our progress towards happiness and need to be tossed out.

Self-searching is a little bit of an oxymoron at this point. As Albert Einstein so eloquently stated, "We can't solve problems by using the same kind of thinking we used when we created them."

Translation: you're going to need help.

"What?" you say. "I thought this was a self-help book!"

The following is probably where most people will stop reading and look for an easier way.

Listen, at some point, if you're really serious about change, you're going to need some help. Crazy, I know. But it's just the way it is. Personally, I use spiritual advisers, life coaches, counselors, therapists, etc. If they have something I think can help me, I use them. There's nothing wrong with asking for help. It's your life, take charge of it.

And, yes, books such as this one can help and provide a road map. But there are some things you just can't get from a book, not even this one. It's the miracle that happens when one human being shares his or her innermost thoughts, fears, and feelings with another.

Many people are reluctant to seek outside help for fear of being judged or they think it shows weakness. But if you find the right person or program, they should be familiar with what you're trying to do and be willing to help. In my experience, it helps to have someone who's not emotionally attached to my situation, someone who can examine my behaviors from an outside perspective without the worry of hurting my feelings. You may be wondering if you can use a friend for this, and while the answer is reluctantly yes, I recommend against it, at least when first starting this process. Since we may still be a little apprehensive about hearing the truth, **it's easy to keep asking different friends until we find someone that co-signs our BS**. Heck, I've been guilty of shopping therapists until I found one that agreed with how great I was, and I was paying them!

I can't tell you who you should seek for guidance in this area. Maybe a therapist, spiritual advisor, clergy, or life coach, but I promise there is someone out there—accessible to you—who can help. Seek and you shall find.

■ Taking an Inventory

As mentioned earlier, self-searching is about making an inventory of character traits, perceptions, and the way we view ourselves and the world we live in——our *way of thinking* that drives us to make certain decisions, decisions that put us in situations or circumstances that continually make us unhappy.

Shouldn't it be simple, if we can recognize our flawed thinking, to just stop thinking that way? After all, knowledge is power! For me, it was not quite that easy. I self-educated for years, but it did not work. I could avoid making the same mistakes or feel good for a period of time—years in some cases—but without an entire psychic change, I eventually found myself in the same state, defeated and depressed.

What I needed was some humility and an honest self-appraisal—humility gained by honestly looking at my life and how I was living it.

This process revealed to me some patterns and areas of interest in my life (these are just a few and are in no particular order):

- ❈ I want to be loved and accepted
- ❈ I am afraid of rejection
- ❈ I do not love myself
- ❈ I am not happy with who I am
- ❈ I am full of guilt and regret
- ❈ I want close relationships, but have no idea how
- ❈ I will never be completely satisfied; thus I am not capable of being happy

If you look at my list, you'll notice some of the items are conflicting.

I want to be loved, yet I am afraid of rejection. Consequently, I never took the chance of finding real love.

I want to be loved but do not love myself. That sure sounds like a tall order, doesn't it?

Sure, people can love me without me loving myself, but to experience the true wonders of love with another human being, I must love and be emotionally connected with self. At least that's been my experience. Not until I learned how to accept and love myself was I truly able to give it away. After all, we can't give away what we do not have. By giving away love, I experience the true beauty of it and am more open to receiving it.

It is important to note that I was not necessarily aware of any of my issues. I just knew I was unfulfilled with life. For the most part, I felt I had a high self-esteem and held a positive self-image. It was months, and in some cases years, before I realized this was not the case.

For example, "I do not love myself." People were always telling me how positive I was and what a great sense of humor I had. I confused looking good on the outside with feeling good on the inside. It was not until years later, once I developed a true loving and empathetic relationship with self through the steps outlined in this book, did I realize what that meant. The process made me realize that if I truly had loved myself, there were things in my past I would not have done. I have come to realize through this process and spiritual growth what a loving relationship with *me* feels like. I can see now that by treating myself the way I did, I was not treating myself as someone I loved.

How you decide to identify and inventory your areas for change may be different, however I do suggest that you ask someone to help you, such as a therapist, chaplain, or someone qualified in self-appraisal.

Again, it helps to look at this process as if you were a storeowner. What products do we have in our inventories that are taking up valuable space? Our inventory is about identifying the items that add value to our lives and those that are causing unhappiness.

■ Inventory Action: Getting it Down on Paper

This is where you take an honest look at yourself. Get out a pen and paper and start writing down things and people you resent and fears you have. Notice I said pen—and not the erasable kind, either! Write down events or things that have happened to you that cause resentment and anger.

Personally, I went back from the time my memory began and wrote down the name of every single person I could remember meeting in my life. That gave me a starting point of seeing if I felt any anger, resentments, or harbored feelings against anyone from my past. After that, I searched my memory for any events that caused me fear, resentment or anger regardless of who was involved. I wrote them down as accurately as I possibly could.

This should also include any sexual experiences that you feel guilt or remorse over. (Honestly, I wrote down everything! Again, I was not qualified to determine which items needed reviewing, so I wrote them all down and let someone more qualified determine which ones needed looking at). Yes, we're talking about sex here. Nothing is held back—you're serious about change, and thus nothing is off limits. It is at this point you truly began getting honest with yourself.

I was amazed at how many sheets of paper I filled. To think that all these years those pages and pages of thoughts had been running rampant through my consciousness. Just think about all that fear, anger, resentment, guilt, and shame running around rent-free in your head, swirling around, feeding off itself.

During this process, we also find that many of these events have taken on a life and story of their own over the years. Meaning that a lot of them, how should I say...were not what actually happened. Over the years, our minds will start to shift and shape events to feed our feelings of fear or insecurities. Why not? After all, we get valuable mileage out of these events during our self-deprecating moments.

Once you have these down on paper, take them to someone who can help determine their meaning or how they're affecting your life today, if at all. For me, I had some sexual things from my early college years that I felt might be hindering my ability to develop intimate relationships. I took my list to my therapist, and we worked through them one by one. Amazingly, some of the issues I thought were significant weren't that meaningful at all, while other, seemingly insignificant events, uncovered areas that I needed to work on.

The amazing thing about this process is we begin to see patterns and themes to our life. We look back and see how we continually placed ourselves in situations to be hurt or unhappy. We may see that we've put unreasonable expectations on ourselves and others and, as a result, were constantly disappointed.

The goal of this process is to rid yourself of those things standing in your way towards happiness. Some call it baggage or character defects. Call it whatever you want, but the reality is, they are getting in your way of powerful life changing growth; both spiritually and emotionally. We must rid ourselves of the obstructions that are getting in the way of our usefulness to our fellow human beings and ourselves.

Chapter 9

Atonement and Forgiveness

"The beauty of life is, while we cannot undo what is done, we can see it, understand it, learn from it, and change. So that every new moment is spent not in regret, guilt, fear, or anger, but in wisdom, understanding, and love."

—*Jennifer Edwards*

The idea of atonement or making restitution can be daunting. Yet if we are serious about finding happiness and our true self, we must rid ourselves of guilt.

Surely all of us at one time or another have done things we're not proud of. Maybe we've hurt someone we love or behaved in a way that brought shame upon ourselves or our family. Regardless of your particular circumstances, you must learn to deal with and move past guilt, resentment, or anger into forgiveness.

This was one of the most difficult areas for me to get past. I had deep guilt and shame about many things in my past. For example: failing as a husband, losing a job, flunking out of college, not being there for a friend when he was dying––the list could go on.

Guilt can be hard to identify at times and manifests itself in many ways. Even though I had guilt or shame swirling around in my head, I was oblivious to the negative effects it was having on my self-esteem. I was pretty good at suppressing and putting on a good façade—mostly to myself—that everything was okay.

Atonement is about making things right with God, others, and ourselves. Yet, just as we cannot give away something we don't have, we cannot make restitution for something we don't understand.

Self-searching and inventory were listed prior to atonement in the sequence of this book for a reason. Identifying and recognizing why we behave a certain way gives perspective to why we may have wronged others or ourselves. This gives meaning and understanding to why we did the things we're shameful about. Even as embarrassing or shameful they make us feel, we have a better understanding of ourselves.

Simply put, we need to know why we are atoning for something for it to have meaning.

It's also important that we don't sacrifice someone else's happiness for our own. We don't apologize or admit to something that may hurt someone else in the process. This is another time when it helps to have a trusted advisor in the matter, someone with a little outside perspective on our situation who can help us determine what (if anything) we need to do to make things right.

"If you believe that you can damage, then believe that you can fix."

——*Rebbe Nachman of Breslov*

■ Forgiveness

Forgiveness is often misunderstood, that by forgiving someone we're suggesting whatever they did was okay. That's not the case, and I'm not going to repeat all the clichés about how forgiveness will set you free. However, I will point out the great effects forgiveness has when dealing with resentments.

A passage from Emmet Fox's *Sermon on the Mount* illustrates this exact point:

Setting others free means setting yourself free, because resentment is really a form of attachment. It is a Cosmic Truth that it takes two to make a prisoner: the prisoner——and a gaoler. There is no such thing as being a prisoner on one's own account. Every prisoner must have a gaoler, and the gaoler is as much a prisoner as his charge. When you hold resentment against anyone, you are bound to that person by a cosmic link, a real, though mental, chain. You are tied by a cosmic tie to the thing that you hate. The one person perhaps in the whole world whom you most dislike is the very one to whom you are attaching yourself by a hook that is stronger than steel. Is this what you wish? Is this the condition in which you desire to go on living? Remember, you belong to the thing with which you are linked in thought, and at some time or other, if that tie endures, the object of your resentment will be drawn again into your life, perhaps to work further havoc. Do you think that you can afford this? Of course, no one can afford such a thing; and so the way is clear. You must cut all such ties, by a clear and spiritual act of forgiveness. You must loose him and let him go. By forgiveness you set yourself free; you save your soul. And because the law of love works alike for one and all, you help to save his soul too, making it just so much easier for him to become what he ought to be.

In order to forgive ourselves, we must rid ourselves of any guilt and resentment that's blocking our progress. We must learn to be honest with ourselves. In order for that to happen, we must share our secrets with someone else.

Yikes! What?

How is telling someone our deepest secrets being honest with ourselves or helping us with forgiveness?

It is the process of saying the words, getting them out into the open, which helps in our healing. By healing our self-image through forgiveness and moving closer to a real perception of ourselves, we move towards truth—truth about ourselves. Not until we truly know who we are, and how we have been affected by our past, can we begin the process of forgiveness and start moving forward into what we might become.

We often find that many of our secrets, things that we secretly condemn ourselves for, are not as bad as they may seem. It is important you share them with someone else for this amazing transformation towards discovering your authentic self and forgiveness to work. So, again, find someone who is familiar with the process and understands what you are trying to accomplish.

Sitting in a room and admitting to the wall my deepest secrets does not accomplish anything. I tried that for years, and nothing happened. Remember, we cannot fix a broken mind with a broken mind. Moreover, we have already accepted something has to change, so we are willing to move forward in the process.

I have used chaplains, life coaches, counselors, and therapists for this process. If you are serious about change, find someone!

I have gone through this process several times, and I can tell you it is not as bad as it seems. In my experience, *thinking* about the wrongs I have done, are causing more soul sickness than the actual acts themselves. It is important that I get them out into the open and discuss them with someone if I am ever going to forgive myself and move on.

The result of this process is a clear and objective look back at the patterns in our lives. This is another reason why we must share our self-searching with another person. The person can help us see events in our past for what they really are—*events in our past.*

Maybe we have been too hard on ourselves for something we have done. Conversely, maybe something happened in our past that is influencing our behavior more than we realize.

My experience with this process has been amazing. The act of sharing my deepest secrets with someone brings me more into the spirit of the universe. It is one step closer to being *a part of* as opposed to *a part from*. When I reach out to another human being and ask for help and guidance, I become receptive to the possibility of miracles and the power of love. True happiness and inner-peace begins with self-acceptance. Self-acceptance begins with forgiveness, forgiveness of oneself. By confessing my faults to someone else, I confess that I am open to the power of forgiveness. It is from this place I have a start for forgiving myself. This makes the process of forgiving others all the more powerful and meaningful.

Only *you* know what you feel guilty for. If you keep guilt and secrets locked away, they'll eat you alive. Trust me; I know that sharing your innermost secrets with another human being can be unthinkable. But I can also share from experience that it's one of the most transformational processes I've ever gone through.

The moment I decided to find happiness, and do whatever possible to make that happen, I stopped caring about what others thought about me. This includes therapists, clergy, coaches, etc. This meant I became willing to be completely honest about what I was feeling and things in my past. By putting my darkest secrets out into the sunlight (sharing them with someone else), they lost some of their hold over me.

One amazing thing about sharing our secrets is we often find them not nearly as bad as we've imagined them in our head. We'll find most are fairly common. Again, we're not that unique in living life and to think that we're the only ones to ever do something we're ashamed of is a pretty narcissistic view.

This is important. There may be some things in your past—like mine—that are pretty scary to share with someone else. Or even things that could possibly get you into real legal trouble. This means you have a right to only share with someone licensed to hear it and more importantly, bound by the law not to disclose anything you've shared with anyone else, i.e. client-patient privilege.

■ Atonement and Forgiveness Actions
Atonement

You're going to need a pen and paper. Start by writing down all the things you feel guilty for. If you're not sure if something is important, write it down anyway. As part of the process, you should share them, as discussed earlier.

Looking over your list, decide (hopefully with the help of someone) if there's anything you can or should do to make things right. Most importantly, **you aren't looking to sacrifice anyone else's happiness to clear your conscience**.

Many things will require no action other than simply not behaving that way again. Others may require an apology or maybe financial restitution. One of my big things was cleaning up my credit history. Another was visiting and apologizing to an old friend who I'd left high-and-dry on a certain job several years earlier.

Deep inside you will know which things weigh heaviest on your conscience. Those are the things that need to be dealt with if humanly possible. In many cases there may be nothing you can do physically or realistically. In these cases, the answer isn't quite so clear. However, if you're sharing what you're going through with someone else, chances are they can help you through it. The most important thing here is to be honest with yourself. Dig deep; more than likely know what needs to be done. And yes, if you're anything like me, it can be a scary affair. But I can attest that after you've done this (and honestly, it's never as bad as the fantasy in our minds), you'll feel a renewed sense of self-worth. This process alone can be life changing.

The important thing here is to clear your conscience— through doing what you know is the right thing— to move forward in your life knowing you've done everything you could to make things right. There isn't any timetable on this, and many things may just be left alone. The important thing is that you can move on with your life and begin leaving this wreckage and baggage behind. You've dealt with it, and it doesn't define you anymore!

■ Forgiveness

Ah, forgiveness. Just the thought of this topic brings light into my soul. Forgiveness has been a huge part of my happiness journey and learning to discover and love my authentic self.

"Forgiveness means giving up all hope for a better past."

—Lily Tomlin

Forgiveness begins with forgiving yourself. If we don't learn how to forgive ourselves, it's difficult, if not impossible, to forgive others. One of the most powerful ways of beginning self-forgiveness is by living right starting today. As you've worked through the previous steps outlined in this book, you should have a better understanding of why you have behaved in a certain way in the past. Hopefully, armed with that knowledge about self, you can start changing and living closer to who you were meant to be.

You are not what you have done in the past. Regardless of your past actions or decisions, believe that you were doing the best you knew how at the time, as was everyone else.

In the next step on spirituality, we'll discuss what I like to call practical prayer. But for an actionable step on forgiveness, I suggest prayer. If you don't believe in prayer, I understand. I was once that way as well, but I strongly suggest keeping an open mind. It will make more sense once you read the next chapter.

If it's someone else you're trying to forgive or have resentments towards, I recommend a common practice suggested in many recovery programs. I can attest that it works.

Pray for the person you resent or need to forgive every night for at least two weeks. And no, however tempting it may be, don't pray they break their leg or go into bankruptcy—I can also attest that doesn't work!

Pray for that person to have all the things you want in your life: love, peace, happiness, and good fortune. That's it. Just put that energy out into the universe, and you'll be amazed with the results.

If it's yourself you really need to forgive, prayer and meditation can also work. However, the best action is to simply start living right. Stop creating wreckage for yourself and others. This is the best way to avoid having to forgive yourself tomorrow for something you've done today.

Chapter 10

Spirituality

Regardless of whether or not you believe in God, Buddha, Allah, higher power, creator of the universe, etc., you can still be a spiritual person. Whether you realize it or not, you probably practice spirituality without even knowing it.

"The definition of spirituality is that which relates to or affects the human spirit or soul as opposed to material or physical things. Spirituality touches that part of you that is not dependent on material things or physical comforts."

——*LivingWordsOfWisdom.com*

Spirituality plays an important part in living a happy life, at least for me and the majority of those I've witnessed who have achieved long-lasting inner-peace and happiness.

This portion of the book is not about discussing theology, but rather about sharing what has worked for me from a practical perspective. I tend to avoid defining my belief as it expands and grows along with my life experience.

The purpose of spirituality in finding happiness is based on a simple concept: *humility*.

■ A Glimpse into the Practicality of Belief

My family attended church every Sunday until I was about five years old——or so I was told, as I vaguely remember. Upon moving to the country so my father could pursue his dream of farming, the church routine stopped.

I do recall having a Bible around the house and that it contained a set of rules by which I was to live. Living in rural Kansas, tornados were common and something my dad found interesting. I recall a steamy summer evening standing next to him on the front porch watching the clouds swirl above our house like an angry toilet bowl. I asked him if he was scared, to which he answered, "It doesn't look good." I guess at ten years old I felt I still had some unfinished business with the man upstairs. That's when my mother found me reading scripture under the table. Even at ten years old, I was foxhole praying.

Growing up, I had no reason to really think about or consider God or spirituality. Honestly, I thought it was something weak people used to make themselves feel better. I do recall loving nature and the wonders of the outdoors. No matter where we lived, my favorite spot was the top of the highest tree, where I would sit for hours and contemplate Earth's beauty and observe the wonders of nature.

My grandfather passed away when I was twenty-two. I remember him being one of the happiest souls I'd known in my inexperienced life. His hickory-striped overalls always hid something fascinating, like a pocket watch and the chain that snuck into the bib pocket just begging us to pull on it. I loved the way he'd say "hot diggity" while slapping his knee, making it impossible to not jump in his lap.

When my grandfather passed, I had a hard time grasping the concept of someone you love being there one day and gone the next. The idea that I would never see him again was difficult to wrap my head around. That was my first glimpse into the possible benefit of religion, spirituality, or a deeper belief system. A reason to believe in something outside of myself and the physical world I lived in. People would say, "He's with God now and resting... He's in a better place." All the time I was thinking, "Good for them, I think that's nice they try to convince themselves he's in heaven so they can feel better." Thinking how foolish it seemed while wishing I could feel better myself.

For the first time I entertained the idea of searching for something to believe in outside of myself. My reasoning was, "If it makes us feel better, why not?" It would be a fleeting glimpse, however, as I set out to conquer and dazzle the world with my amazing abilities and charisma. Deep down in my core, I believed there was nothing out there beyond what I could see or touch, so I'd better go get as much of it as I could.

Thirteen years later, I realized I would need to believe in something besides myself if I wanted to live. It was then—out of desperation—I went searching for something.

That *something* has turned into an important part of living a happy life. Just as I choose to see the good in other people, I choose to believe there is something outside of myself that I can rely on for strength and guidance.

There's a line from Brennan Manning's book *The Ragamuffin Gospel* that's always resonated with me: "It is not objective proof of God's existence that we want but the experience of God's presence."

My God is in the mud; she was there with me. I don't understand the Divine; I don't need to. I do know the loving spirit that guides me, provides for me, if and when I open myself up to the possibility. I can't deny it; I experience it everyday. I experience it through miracles happening in people's lives. I see it in the homeless man's face standing on the street corner. I am him. I see it in the mother addicted to crack grasping for a reason to live. I am her. When I see these people open their hearts to the possibility of something more powerful than themselves, and they begin cultivating self-worth and purpose in life, I experience God, the Divine, something more powerful than myself.

Call it law of attraction, the spirit of the universe, whatever, I don't care what it is or need to define it; I just open myself to the possibility of it and experience it.

■ Believing Versus Knowing

After my father's sudden death in 2010, I was reminded again—up close and personal—of my own mortality. The experience reminded me of what I felt as a twenty-two-year-old about my grandfather's death. Moreover, will all the work I've done and spiritual progress I've made since help me when I need it the most? Or am I just preparing to shield myself from reality when something really tragic happens?

Do I really believe or know everything will be okay?

At this stage in my spiritual journey, I mostly believe. But as I experience more of life and remain conscious throughout each experience—allowing them to take me to where I'm supposed to be—I begin to know.

Early in my spiritual journey I believed certain things because I witnessed them happening in the lives of others. The seed began with the simple belief that if it could happen for them, maybe it could happen for me. Things like practical prayer: that by praying for others more than myself, I was consciously thinking of others more and I would eventually become less selfish. Moreover, I began to witness others go through tragic experiences with grace while maintaining a sense of inner-peace and serenity.

Just because we believe in some higher power or become spiritual does not mean we avoid suffering or pain. Quite contrary, Buddhism suggests that suffering is an essential part of life. From *Mindfulness in Plain English* by Bhante Henepola Gunaratana:

The essence of life is suffering, said the Buddha. At first glance this seems exceedingly morbid and pessimistic. It even seems untrue. After all, there are plenty of times when we are happy. Aren't there? No, there are not. It just seems that way. Take any moment when you feel really fulfilled and examine it closely. Down under the joy, you will find that subtle, all-pervasive undercurrent of tension that, no matter how great the moment is, it is going to end. No matter how much you just gained, you are either going to lose some of it or spend the rest of your days guarding what you have got and scheming how to get more. And in the end, you are going to die. In the end, you lose everything. It is all transitory.

Sounds pretty bleak, doesn't it? Luckily, it's not—not at all. It only sounds bleak when you view it from the ordinary mental perspective, the very perspective at which the treadmill mechanism operates. Underneath lies another perspective, a completely different way to look at the universe. It is a level of functioning in which the mind does not try to freeze time, does not grasp onto our experiences as it flows by, and does not try to block things out and ignore them. It is a level of experience beyond good and bad, beyond pleasure and pain. It is a lovely way to perceive the world, and it is a learnable skill. It is not easy, but it can be learned.

The essence of spirituality for me has been to learn how to manifest an underlying belief system that is based on experience and keeps me in the moment.

So the key to managing suffering is to discover this thing called *spirituality* and the ability to match calamity with serenity, working towards inner-peace and the ability to stay as present in each moment as possible. We begin to realize the spiritual power of now. That is precisely what the previous steps in this process are about, clearing away the garbage—regrets, guilt, fear, etc.—swirling in our heads that keeps us out of the present moment or awake at night.

■ Practical Prayer

I work with computers. I like things that make sense, most of the time. As a kid, I was always taking things apart—clocks, radios, you name it—to discover what made them tick. I sought logical explanations for everything.

It was first suggested by a mentor years ago that I get on my knees and pray every morning and night. My response was, "I'm not sure I believe in God, so what's the use?" His response, "Jared, I didn't ask you what you believed in, I asked you to pray. It's not always about you or what you believe. Just do it."

I was desperate enough to try anything, so reluctantly I followed his suggestion. As a newbie to prayer, I was told to keep it simple and to follow a few guidelines:

- ❀ In the morning ask for guidance.
- ❀ At night, give thanks.

* Never ask for anything for yourself other than guidance.

* Always pray for others.

* Never pray for patience, as you will inevitably be tested for it. But rather pray for acceptance.

So that's how I started praying. In the morning I'd pray to *nothing* for guidance and at night—again to *nothing*—say thanks. I say *nothing*, yet I did have some belief in the man who was suggesting I do this. He was real and seemed happy. I believed that if it worked for him, just maybe it could work for me, too.

I continued this every morning and night for about a year. Praying for others, praying that people other than me have love, happiness, and health in their lives. I prayed for specific people, people I knew were struggling with personal problems or illness. I prayed for people I resented, that they have the same things I would want for myself. Things like love, happiness, prosperity, and even specifics such as a family and a good job.

One evening on the way home from work, an accident caused four lanes of traffic to come to a dead standstill. Of course this was the night I was to meet my new girlfriend out for dinner. Having driven this commute for several months now, I knew my normal forty-minute commute was now easily going to be two hours. I felt the aggravation start to swell up in my chest as I thought about pounding on the steering wheel. *Then a miracle happened.* My next thought went to the people in the accident, my heart swelled for them and their family members, and I began to pray for them. Calmness came over me as I prayed for those in the accident and their families. However long it would take me to get home would be nothing compared to the sadness one would feel if their loved one just died on this highway. As I looked around at the other drivers beating on their steering wheels in frustration, I realized *I had changed*.

Today I do believe in a power greater than myself—which I call God. Whether it is God, Jehovah, Allah, Shiva, Brahma, Vishnu, or Zeus, to me it doesn't matter. In the words of Elizabeth Gilbert from *Eat, Pray, Love*, "I have nothing against these terms. I feel they are all equal because they are all equally adequate and inadequate descriptions of the indescribable. But we each do need a functional name for this indescribability, and 'God' is the name that feels the most warm to me, so that's what I use."

As a practical person, I realized I had changed through the practice of prayer. At times I overanalyze the use of prayer, telling myself I'm simply more thoughtful of others because I'm taking the action of praying for them more. But in the end, it all comes down to action. I take the action and *something*, practical or not, happens. I simply had to commit to something long enough to experience a power greater than myself.

One simple prayer I still use every morning is, "God, show me what you will have me do today, and give me the strength and willingness to carry it out."

By saying this prayer, I am asking for guidance. As a result, I'm more aware throughout the day of opportunities I'm presented to be of service. Then I get to see how serious I am about taking action.

As you know, I'm big on action. One action I take when praying is to get on my knees. In the morning it's in the closet right before I put on my pants. Yes, one leg at a time. In the evening it's next to my bed. The action for me is about humility. Plus, I'm a typical man and can be a little superstitious and routine oriented. Sort of like wearing my lucky underwear when going to job interviews... Okay, not like that but sort of.

Spirituality Action

Anyone, regardless of beliefs, can practice spirituality. In essence, spirituality is a quest for self-transformation.

■ Six Ways You Can Practice Spirituality

1. Learning the True Nature of Self

By looking deep inside ourselves, we begin to understand how we operate. We can take a close look at our fears—rejection, abandonment, failure, success—and things that throw us off balance. Then we're able to search for the cause in underlying emotions.

The truth is most people find the same things underneath; further evidence that we're all linked in one form or another and more similar than our egos would have us believe.

As we learn more about ourselves, we're better equipped to understand others. This leads to open-mindedness, forgiveness, and empathy.

2. Make a Choice

Self-transformation begins with a choice, a decision to seek a more spiritual life.

"When the student is ready, the teacher will appear."

——Buddhist Proverb

The fact that you're reading this book means you're seeking something. We all have to start somewhere. The important thing is to keep searching until you find something that makes sense to you. The choice is yours; take what you need and leave the rest.

3. Self-Help/Personal Development

Have you checked out the self-help or personal development section at your local book store lately? (Chances are you have since you're reading this book—thanks again by the way). It's packed full of all sorts of topics; many of which touch on spirituality in one form or another. A few books I highly recommend are *There's a Spiritual Solution to Every Problem* by Dr. Wayne Dyer and *The Sermon on the Mount: The Key to Success in Life* by Emmet Fox.

4. Meditation

There are many forms of meditation. Find one that works for you. Try to keep it simple in the beginning until you find something that works. One technique I use often is simple breathing. Taking long breaths; I think the word *God* when breathing in and *self* upon breathing out. I have a ritual of doing this in the hot tub after a run or workout.

For a good starting point, check out http://jaredakers. com/meditation

5. Ask for Guidance

Find someone who has something you want spiritually, and ask them how they got there. There are spiritual coaches and programs that help people live more spiritual lives. Again, it's important to find something that makes sense to you; listen to your gut.

Personal development guru Steve Pavlina, in his article, "How To Graduate From Christianity," says, "When you see enforcement based on the promise of rewards and punishments, you're not witnessing real truth. You're witnessing marketing masquerading as truth."

6. Exercise

Spirituality has nothing to do with materialism or our physical comforts; it touches on mind, body, and spirit. As the other five points deal mostly with mind and spirit, exercising the body is spiritual.

Once you start taking care of your mind and spirit, you'll intuitively want to live a healthier lifestyle physically.

Most people cannot deny the power behind a healthy body, mind, and spirit. It sort of reminds me of my first car, a maroon Oldsmobile Cutlass Supreme Classic. It was a project car of a nearby high school. It looked cool as hell, but the engine was crap! It doesn't matter how good you look if you can't get to where you need to go.

The most important thing about spirituality is to seek something, and **don't stop until the miracle happens**.

Chapter 11

Maintenance

After going through the previous six steps, a transformation should begin to happen. We have felt our existence come into peace with the world around us. We can look the world in the eye and know that we have done the best we can. We feel that we are a part of something now, something bigger than ourselves. For we have laid the foundation with which real spiritual growth and happiness will spring.

We have learned:

Step 1: In Awareness, we became aware that, if we are not satisfied with the way things are, change is needed to find true inner-peace and happiness.

Step 2: In Surrender, we learn to give up control and stop fighting. Conversely, we learn we have a lot of control over ourselves and that we can stop being a victim.

Step 3: Acceptance taught us about accepting the things we can change: ourselves. And that we are responsible for becoming what we dream of becoming.

Step 4: Self-Searching and Inventory Management is where we learned how to identify the things that we must change, things that keep us from growing spiritually and towards inner-peace and happiness. This is where we discovered the how and why of our past behaviors.

Step 5: Atonement and Forgiveness taught us humility, making things right, and forgiveness. We learn to do the right thing and make reparations for past wrongs. We make right, if at all possible, those things that keep us awake at night.

Step 6: Spirituality is where we start putting into practice things like meditation and prayer. Even if we don't believe in something, we can start somewhere and continually seek. If anything, we can accept the logic behind practical prayer, that praying for others will help us become less self-centered.

We have cleared, or at least started to clear, the things from our past that have kept us awake at night and stolen our peace of mind. This means that we can now walk upright, with pride and dignity. If there are things that continue to nudge our conscience, that keep our eyes looking down, we must be willing to take more action to make things right where possible. This may mean more work on forgiveness or atonement towards self and others.

Nothing is too great a task, for we are on a path to true happiness. And it is ours to claim.

Remember our quote:

"Happiness is when what you think, what you say, and what you do are in harmony."

——Ghandi

Is this not what we have done?

Looking back when we started, we realized we needed to get three things in harmony to find happiness: thought, actions, and words. The first four steps were all about getting our thinking (thought) straight. Steps 5 and 6 are where we began the path of doing the right thing (actions). The by-product of having a clear conscience and right living is that we no longer need validation and happiness from outside ourselves. What others do or think is no longer our biggest concern, but rather how we are living. We are being true to ourselves and our highest ideals.

We find that we no longer need to say (words) or do things that are harmful to others. Actions and words used only to hurt others and inflate ourselves are no longer needed. For everything we need is within us as individuals, given to us by our creator.

Maintenance is about living each day to the best of our ability. Having followed these steps, we can move forward knowing we have done the best we can. So each day we set out to bring joy and love to the lives of others. As a friend of mine says, "Today, I will only give and receive love."

Here are a few maintenance steps I do on a daily basis. Each morning when I wake, I do four things before starting my day:

1. Take a shower
2. Get on my knees
3. Pray - Before I get off my knees, I remain quiet and just sit there for several minutes and listen to the day begin. I make sure I'm ready for the day and that I will be open to all possibilities
4. Read one of my morning meditation/affirmation books

At night before going to bed, I again do four things:

1. Brush my teeth
2. Get on my knees
3. Pray
4. Kiss my wife

My nightly prayer consists of thanks mostly. I also do sort of a mental recap of my day, going over the entire day in my head to see if there are any areas that I can improve upon. I think about others who I know are suffering or struggling, and I pray for them. This is also when I pray for those I may have resentment towards. I pray that they have all of the things in their lives that I want in mine: happiness, love, joy, health, and peace. If there is something going on in my life that's causing me worries (e.g. new job, Dr's appointment, etc.), I pray for acceptance of the outcome whatever it may be.

You may wonder why I put "get on my knees" in both lists as something I do—and not just prayer. As mentioned earlier, I originally started doing it because it was suggested by someone I admired. It was a symbol of my willingness to change. Now I do it because hitting my knees is an action. It forces me to concentrate on what I'm doing and is a physical display of humility and gratitude.

"We must never forget that it is through our actions,
words, and thoughts that we have a choice."

—*Sogyal Rinpoche*

■ Maintenance Actions

Having worked through the steps in this book, daily maintenance is fairly easy—comparatively.

In essence, you will work through each of these steps every day. Over time, it will become natural and something you do without even thinking about it.

Since you no longer require external validation to feel good about yourself—because you know in your heart you are living true to self—your tongue will be more restrained. You won't need to lash out at others or feel resentment, for you've accepted what you can and cannot control.

It's been my experience, that by continually working on my spiritual growth through daily maintenance, I have a constant pulse on where I'm at emotionally. This allows me to deal with just about anything in life. However, even in times of great trials, I'm still open to seeking help by visiting my therapists or seeking help in other areas.

Part IV: A New Perspective

"My friend Joe Mathews shared a poignant story with me recently. His best friend's wife was diagnosed with terminal cancer and given a short time to live. Joe said he watched in awe as Dan and his wife, Christine, began to live each day with tremendous clarity and love. When it was nearly the end Joe finally got up the courage to ask Christine the question: 'What does it feel like to live each day knowing you are dying?' She raised herself up on one arm, and then asked him, 'Joe, what does it feel like to live each day pretending that you are not?'"

——From Jesus, Life Coach by Laurie Beth Jones

Chapter 12

Dealing with Unhappy People

"Before you diagnose yourself with depression or low self-esteem, first make sure that you are not, in fact, just surrounded by assholes."

——*William Gibson*

We all know someone who's a real drag. There's constant drama going on in their lives, as every other week they're in a new relationship or dealing with some tragic event in their lives. Maybe that's you?

You care about them and hope they find what they're looking for. But sometimes you just get sick and tired of hearing the same thing over and over. Don't you? What do you do then?

The easiest thing to do is avoid them. Of course that's not realistic in most cases...or is it?

We have a choice about who we allow in our lives. If someone is causing us stress and unhappiness, we can cut them off. I know you probably can't believe I'm saying this. And of course the obvious question is: what if I'm married to one?

I get a lot of emails from people around the world who subscribe to my newsletter via my website asking these exact questions. Having been in a few unhealthy relationships myself (which is an entirely different book), I know that it can be hard to deal with people who become emotional black holes in our lives. But *we* give them the power to suck us dry. Maybe that sounds harsh, but it was certainly true in my case. It didn't matter who I was with, if I wasn't happy with myself, nothing external was going to change that. However, that's not to say a spouse or family member can't severely hinder your journey towards happiness. In any case, all you can ever really do is work on yourself.

This deals with the concept of control: as in, what can we really control? Logically we can accept the only control we have is of ourselves. So even in these instances that's where we need to focus.

Think about the last time anyone ever really changed your mind about something. I mean completely changed the way you perceived something that you knew, deep in your soul, was a certain way. Has it ever happened, honestly? Has someone changed your mind or the way you act simply because they continually nagged you about it? I would bet almost never.

So how likely are you to cause profound changes in someone by focusing more on them?

As the saying goes, "Be the change you want to see in the world."

The most significant, long-lasting, and internal change occurs when people decide they want something for themselves. Maybe they've witnessed the change in you, that you've found some form of peace and happiness. Situations that used to upset you no longer get under your skin. Hopefully it moves them to want what you have. And they ask how you got there. Or they resent you more for it and become more difficult to be around or stay the same. Either way, you continue your journey towards happiness.

It's like when airline stewardesses instruct you to put the oxygen mask on yourself before your child. If you're unhappy and not taking care of yourself first, you're no good to anyone.

It is important, however, to be cognizant of our motives. If we're acting a certain way with the motive of changing the other person rather than concentrating on ourselves, we're still under the illusion of control.

Be a beacon of hope. Loving proof that happiness exists. There may come a time when a tough decision needs to be made——whether to stay in a relationship or leave? At what point is our own happiness worth sacrificing for the sake of a relationship or commitment?

That's a tough question and one that's hard to provide any real answer to. There are so many variables that would play into that question, like motives or rationalization, to just name a few. If I'm not clear with who I am and love and respect self, I can rationalize anything to feed my ego. The man I am today would not be in most of the relationships I was in before. I'm a completely different person today.

But what about family members we don't necessarily live with? In that case, just avoid it.

Maybe avoiding family members who irritate or make us unhappy seems obvious, and to some, selfish; but let's think about it. Remember that you are not responsible for someone else's feelings. With that said, you should never do something that deliberately hurts someone, either. Nonetheless, we all have a right to say no.

It's no big secret that family causes a lot of stress and unhappiness in people's lives. And it's common to hear people say family is the most important thing. But that's also easy for most of us to say when we have family. The least we can do is suffer through the resentment and guilt only family members know how to inflict. After all, we hurt the ones we love. But at what point do we stop trying to improve relationships, family or not, that do not add real value to our lives or grow in a positive direction? That question really becomes hard when dealing with family.

But isn't family about unconditional love and being there no matter what? To some extent, yes. But you can love without caring. Something Martha Beck discussed in her article "How to Love More by Caring Less" in the July 2011 issue of *O, The Oprah Magazine*:

...I've found that loving without caring is a useful approach—I'd venture to say the best approach—in most relationships, especially families.

To care for someone can mean to adore them, feed them, tend their wounds. But care can also signify sorrow, as in "bowed down by cares." Or anxiety, as in "Careful!" Or investment in an outcome, as in "Who cares?" The word love has no such range of meaning: It's pure acceptance.

For you, loving without caring might mean staying calm when your sister gets divorced, or your dad starts smoking again, or your husband is laid off.

You may think that in such situations not getting upset would be unloving. But consider: If you were physically injured, bleeding out, would you rather be with someone who screamed and swooned, or someone who stayed calm enough to improvise a tourniquet?

Real healing, real love comes from people who are both totally committed to helping—and able to emotionally detach.

This is because, on an emotional level, our brains are designed to mirror one another. As a result, when we're anxious and controlling, other people don't respond with compliance; they reflect us by becoming—press the button when you get the right answer— anxious and controlling. Anger elicits anger, fear elicits fear, no matter how well meaning we may be.

It's easier to emotionally detach when we know our happiness is not contingent on others. This becomes possible through loving and accepting our authentic self.

■ Have a Plan for the Drama Queens

To some people, drama is like oxygen. You know the ones who just can't help themselves. The uncle who constantly brings up the time he bailed you out of jail or friend who just can't seem to get a break in life. Family members know how to push our buttons better than anyone else. But when the zingers start flying, you have a choice to participate or not. The best way to deal with these situations when they can't be avoided is come up with a plan.

Decide beforehand how you're going to handle the uncomfortable situations that always seem to get to you. Talk about your strategy with your spouse, friend, therapist, coach, or other family members. If avoidance is not an option, being prepared is the best way to handle stressful situations with grace and dignity. One of the best ways of diffusing uncomfortable situations is with kindness. If your uncle brings up the time he bailed you out of jail, tell him thanks and that you really appreciated him being there for you. And avoid the sarcasm. No, my uncle never bailed me out of jail… Not that I wasn't ever in jail, but it was my dad who had to come get me. Thank God for small towns.

Maybe it becomes more of a challenge when you have children. Although I don't have biological children, I have been blessed with a granddaughter—due to my wife's previous marriage—and stepson and stepdaughter, whom I love. It makes me feel good when they want to hang out with us and stop by to visit or stay for dinner. When dealing with family or friends, try to remember: "Be understanding rather than understood." Try to understand where your mother-in-law or parents are coming from when they insist you come to visit or rearrange the knickknacks in your living room every time they stop by. At any given time, we're all doing the best we know how.

Sometimes we just have to remind ourselves that we're grown-ups and can do what we want. This can be hard when our family members can still push those guilt buttons. A good test is to think about what memories you have or will have of times spent with loved ones. Will they be good ones?

We have the right to surround ourselves with people who inspire us. And that goes for family members as well. The more you discover and love your authentic self, the more in tune you'll become to what effects (negative and positive) external forces are having on your happiness. From then on, it becomes easier to avoid the emotional black holes in your life. You'll also discover that as you become happier and at peace with yourself, you attract similar people. That's something I've really noticed the last couple of years. My wife and I have a very small circle of friends, but the ones we do have add positive energy to our lives. You should gravitate towards those who inspire you, not tire you.

■ Surround Yourself with Positive Energy

In Wayne Dyer's book *There's A Spiritual Solution To Every Problem,* he suggests that we "think of energy in a context of vibration and movement." He goes on to say, "You have within you the absolute ability to increase your frequency and enhance the energy field of your everyday life. By increasing the speed at which you vibrate, you move into those frequencies I am calling spirit and away from those that are grounded in the material world of problems."

It makes sense that we are attracted to people who seem to have higher energy. Or according to Wayne Dyer, have faster vibrations and are closer to "spirit." He explains this:

Think about what it is like to be around people who seem to posses these highest capacities of the mind. When we observe someone who has deep insight we can become easily transfixed. The person of deep insight who touches your soul with his words and ignites feelings of love and appreciation is vibrating at a faster energy frequency.

This is why we're attracted to people who inspire us with their enlightenment, loving hearts, and positive energy. Additionally, people with negative energy can bring us down. Here's another except from Wayne Dyer on this topic:

...the faster vibrations of surrender, love, relationship to the infinite, quiet emptiness, generosity, and gratitude, feeling connected rather separate, and finally a sense of cheerfulness. These are my [Wayne Dyer] definitions and they could include many subareas such as faith, hope, patience, sympathy, kindness, forgiveness, and noninterference.

It is these faster frequencies that you will be brining to the front door of your life and filling every room with until there is no longer any space for those slower vibrations that seemed to fill your house with problems. The slowed-down frequencies are the obstacles. They will depart when you bring the vibrational world of spirit into their presence.

Personally, I believe that these negative energies can exist in many areas. Although it all may sound a little hokey to some, the evidence in my life has been substantial, from simple things like not watching the local news, where "if it bleeds, it leads" is a constant reminder of all the terrible things people are doing to one another. By not watching the news or movies that portray too much violence, I try to limit the amount of negative energy in my life. And that goes for negative people as well. Many believe that these negative effects can be harmful not only in our immediate physical presence, but out into our neighborhoods and communities as well.

On a side note: I've dreamed of starting a media network that focuses completely on positive things happening in our local communities. There are miracles happening all around us that get drowned out by all the violence. Unfortunately, the advertising dollars follow the eyeballs, and until people start demanding positive media, it would have to be a completely self-funded network.

In my experience, the more positive energy I begin to manifest from within self, the more positive people and experiences I attract, and conversely, the less receptive I am of people, places, or things that harbor negativity. There's an entire industry devoted to this concept of the law of attraction. And yes, I believe in it, but I think a lot of people bought into the *secret* that I can just sit around and think positive things and my life will get better. As I've mentioned before, nothing ever happened to me by just sitting around thinking about it. I didn't experience any of these positive affects until after I did the work outlined in this book.

Simply cutting out the unhappy people from your life may not be realistic. But you may be surprised at how few people you really need in your life. I'm not saying become introverted and shut out anyone you dislike (trust me; I tried that for years, too). Often the people who annoy us the most are our best teachers. There's a common belief that if there's something about a particular person you don't like, it's a reflection of something in yourself. It sounds pretty introspective, but I'm not completely sold on that theory yet. At least I don't have enough personal experience to write anything in depth about it. It's just something to think about.

Even if you can't distance yourself completely from the negative people in your life, you can set limits and boundaries. Being a shoulder to cry on is noble, but when your friend is using your shoulder as a life preserver to avoid taking responsibility for his or her own actions, you're not helping much either. It's okay to set boundaries, practice some "tough love," or detach a little. Explain to them that you'll love them regardless of what happens, but they need to seek the answers for themselves. In many cases, maybe they have asked you for advice, you've given it, and they continue to put themselves in bad situations.

At some point you have to realize there's only so much you can do. Again, you can't help someone who doesn't want help. The best thing is to constantly let them know you love them. And if it were me, I'd pray for them also; put some positive energy out in the universe for them.

Chapter 13

Be Like A Tree

As a zookeeper back in the early '90s, each spring it was my job to round up our spider monkey troop and transport them to their outdoor enclosure for the summer. It was exciting, or should have been for the spider monkeys. After all, they'd get to swing from real trees, frolic in the grass, and do all of the things that spider monkeys naturally do.

It was my first year, and as the new guy, I was simply handed a large dog kennel, a net, and told to hop in the cage and catch me a spider monkey. As the gate closed and latched behind me, I heard the elder keeper say, "Oh, this is important: if you happen to trap a spider monkey, especially the male Carlos, on the ground with the net and you see he's about to get loose, just let go of the net and get out of the way." Okay… "Why's that?" I asked. "Well, they feel pretty vulnerable when on the ground and will seek high ground for safety. This means they'll climb anything, including you…and they have pretty nasty canines."

Outstanding.

So there I stood, armed with a net and locked in a small space with five scared and screaming spider monkeys. Maybe you've heard the phrase, "I'll come at you like a spider monkey"? Well, I'll just say spider monkeys are deceptively strong little things and aren't too fond of being chased around with a net. Plus, they have a prehensile tail, giving them five good arms to resist with. Netting one is like trying to hold a large beach ball underwater.

That was the first time I heard, up close and personal, the distinct distress call of a male spider monkey. It's pretty impressive, particularly when heard about three inches from your face while being shaken by your shirt collar. I concur that indeed they have large canines, as well as horrible breath—at least Carlos did.

After that circus act, someone suggested a better way. Apparently they'll run right into the dog kennel if you fill it full of monkey biscuits and place it right outside their sliding den door. Slide the door open, and they run right in.

The spider monkeys resisted because they didn't know what we knew. They couldn't see the wonderful place we were taking them. They felt comfortable where they were but didn't realize there was this amazing place they would love much better.

In late summer of 2006, I was lying in the grass at a park looking up at a tree and pondering what God's will was for me. I noticed how the tree branches would be going one direction then shoot off in another. What made them do that? What force made them go in a certain direction? Then I realized a tree is just a tree. **It's being exactly what God intends it to be, its authentic self.** It's strong and provides shelter and food for everyone around it, just by being what it's intended to be. It's not trying to be a rock star or grape bush; it's just being the best tree it knows how to be.

For years I was like the spider monkeys, freaking out every time life threw me a curve and wondering what the hell was going on. I didn't realize God had a wonderful place he wanted me to be. A beautiful world where I could be free and do all the wonderful things that makes life so beautiful—like love and be loved. I just couldn't see it. I was too busy trying to be a rock star.

So today I'm just trying to be the best *me* I can be. Let life take me to where I'm supposed to be and not just where I've ended up. To be the best human I can be, who can love and be loved. More like a tree.

We already have everything we need to be happy. We were born with it. Just as the apple seed has everything it needs to sprout, take root, flower, and produce apples, you have everything you need to be whole and happy. You just need to believe it, nurture it, allow it to take root, and give it all the love and attention it needs to grow and produce wonderful fruit.

The authentic you *is* beautiful. Believe it.

Chapter 14

Happiness in Spite of Life

To be really happy all the time is unrealistic. However, it's not unrealistic to live with an underlying belief—a foundational knowing—that everything is fundamentally going to be okay.

Finding that foundation of inner-peace comes from discovering your authentic self and knowing that it's enough.

> *"When you realize there is nothing lacking, the whole world belongs to you."*

—*Lao Tzu*

■ Living True to Self

I recall an allergy commercial on TV where a man is walking through the woods. There are two separate versions of him, both slightly transparent as they walk along separate paths. After taking the allergy medicine, the two versions combine into one clear representation of a man as he begins walking along a well-defined and clear path. I feel that's what's happened to me. Before this process, I was split into two incomplete versions of self—one version consisting of my ego and what I showed to the world, the other a lost soul wandering aimlessly through life.

Today I am whole.

Since that day in March of 2006, I've accomplished a lot. I've finished my undergraduate degree in Information Technology and went on to complete an MBA. Not bad for guy who flunked out of college the first time around. And last year I also fulfilled a lifelong dream of competing in a few short-course triathlons. It's amazing what you can accomplish one step at a time.

"Men do not attract that which they want, but that which they are."

—*James Allen (As A Man Thinketh)*

After eleven months of working on myself—at age thirty-six—I met my wife, Emily. Having been through some difficult circumstances in her life, she had gone through a transformation as well. Together, we've lived out a common dream of becoming certified SCUBA divers and traveling as much as possible. The most amazing part about our relationship is the respect we have for ourselves as individuals first, which strengthens our love and respect for each other.

When I met Emily, I wasn't sure if I would ever have children or if I wanted them at all. I was just learning who I was and how to love myself. So I prayed about it, turning it over just like everything else. In April of 2009, Emily's son and his wife had a baby girl, making me a thirty-eight-year-old grandpa at the time. Pretty cool.

My deepest wish is that you discover and love your authentic self. After that, everything else is just gravy.

■ Make Happy Memories

It was a beautiful summer day in 2007. Emily and I were still dating at the time and were visiting her son and his wife. They own a small house in a rural town about twenty minutes away. It was to be a short visit, just to drop off a paint sprayer we bought for them. They were in the process of painting their house, and this was sort of our way of getting out of helping—by purchasing them a nice paint sprayer (at least that's the way my selfish brain saw it). I had visions of spending the rest of the afternoon lounging by a pool doing nothing. It was going to be great.

We arrived with the paint sprayer to discover they really didn't want it or need it, really. *Well, okay*, I thought, *we tried*. Then Emily, out of nowhere, offered our labor and painting services for the rest of the afternoon. I felt the resentment rise up inside me as I saw my lazy afternoon quickly dissolve into hours of sweat and climbing up and down ladders. I recognized what was happening so I left the room and went outside. I found a quiet place by a tree, sat down, and prayed. I asked for acceptance and the willingness to do what was right and from a place of love. Then, it came to me. Years from now, will I remember the day I sat by the pool and did nothing, or the day I helped my girlfriend's son and his wife paint their house? The answer was clear, and it felt great! We spent the rest of the afternoon painting their house.

Years from now, we're more likely to remember a day spent helping someone else. Happy people make happy memories.

■ Being of Service and Gratitude

Being of service is one of the greatest callings there is. When all else fails, when nothing else seems to get me out of my funky mood, helping someone else seems to always be what I need.

From the movie *Peaceful Warrior*:
Dan: Hey Socrates, if you know so much, why are you working at a gas station?
Socrates: It's a service station. We offer service. There's no higher purpose.
Dan: ...than pumping gas?
Socrates: Service to others.

And, yes, there are times when I just seem to get a little down. Like just recently, my wife and I had just finished dinner and I was downstairs watching TV when I was consumed with this overall feeling of dread. Real doom and gloom from out of nowhere. I could not put my finger on the reason why, but I was overcome with this feeling of hopelessness and that something in the universe was not right. There was a disturbance in my soul, or as Obi-Wan put it, "I felt a great disturbance in the Force, as if millions of voices suddenly cried out in terror and were suddenly silenced. I fear something terrible has happened." Okay, that's a little dramatic, but sometimes it can certainly feel that way when you're normally brimming with gratitude.

So I lay back on the couch and just felt it. I considered grabbing a pen and paper and writing a gratitude list, knowing the action would help and then I could share how I "walk the walk." But I didn't; instead I used the power of now and then went through a mental list of all that I was grateful for such as my wife, granddaughter, mother, job, legs, food, home, etc. and that all my basic needs were met. I know I talk about gratitude a lot, but it is important.

"Gratitude unlocks the fullness of life. It turns what we have into enough, and more. It turns denial into acceptance, chaos to order, confusion to clarity. It can turn a meal into a feast, a house into a home, a stranger into a friend. Gratitude makes sense of our past, brings peace for today, and creates a vision for tomorrow."

——Melody Beattie

Chris Guillebeau of *The Art of Nonconformity*, listed three parts of gratitude in his ZenHabits.net guest post, "Three Truths to Help You Create a Life of Gratitude."

A life of gratitude is composed of three parts that combine to make a whole.

1. A sense of purpose in our lives

2. An appreciation for the lives of those around us
3. A willingness to take action to show the gratitude we feel

■ Finding A Sense of Purpose

Finding a sense of purpose in one's life is no small task. For most of my life, I thought "the purpose" was to find happiness. This thinking simply brought on years of self-will and wrestling with most forces in life. Through the gift of desperation, I realized a life run on self-will alone puts me in conflict with the universe and everyone in it. Think about it——if we're all trying to run our lives on self-will, getting the most out of life for ourselves, who's looking out for each other?

It's like when my wife and I go to Home Depot on the weekends. It's really quite funny. We get all dressed up and looking nice just in case someone sees us. I mean, really! Isn't everyone else just going around doing the same thing—wondering how everyone sees them? The good thing is we're able to laugh at ourselves about it.

Finding a sense of purpose can be as easy as doing what makes you happy. I found mine after working through the process in this book and finding that living a life based on spiritual principles and helping others as much as I can makes me happy. I used to think I had to change the world, you know, really make a difference! Today I can search for my life purpose each and every day. My morning prayer is, "God, show me what you will have me do today and give me the strength and willingness to carry it out." When I approach each day with this attitude, anything is possible!

■ Appreciate Those Around You

Appreciation is an action; look at those around you in everyday life and see what you can do to make their lives better. Here's something to try. The next time you feel frustrated, angry, or upset because you feel someone just doesn't understand, try being understanding rather than understood.

Bringing joy to those around you is a great way to show your appreciation for them. One of my favorite parts of the movie *The Bucket List* is when Carter poses the two questions that are asked of Egyptians entering heaven: "Have you found joy in your life?" and "Has your life brought joy to others?" Bring joy to others, and you'll find joy yourself.

■ Gratitude is an Action

I love it, just love it—anything to do with action! I used to think about getting flowers or a gift for someone, but never really took any action. I was too busy changing the world. People's happiness comes from my actions, not my intentions. It is simple—doing things for others shows them you appreciate them.

There are so many ways you can take action to show gratitude, such as how you treat yourself and your possessions. Are you grateful for your life and your body?

Try exercising. Are you grateful for your car? Try washing it. Are you grateful for your clothes? …Okay, I didn't really think "try washing them" would be that impactful, so how about this: if you're grateful for having more than enough clothes, give some of them away to a local shelter.

As I lay there on the couch and thought of all that I am grateful for, the feeling of dread lifted just a little. I got on my knees and said a simple prayer, "God, thank you for your grace and confidence," and went upstairs to share my feelings with my wife. (I share everything; it's good practice for when I'm making unreasonable demands of myself) She kissed me and told me she loves me—it lifted a little more.

From experience I know that emotions are just emotions, that they change, and that *this too shall pass*. The next morning I rise and am grateful for another day as a flower is for the sun.

■ Emotional Connectedness

Becoming emotionally connected to self as a result of the process outlined in this book has been one of the most critical elements to my sustained happiness. I can identify the underlying emotions of any discomfort, deal with it, and move on. Conversely, I get to revel in the realness and warmth of all positive emotions as well.

More important is the knowing that I can feel an emotion completely, let it take me to where I'm supposed to go, and come out on the other side—still happy, still loved, and at peace with myself and the world. That's pretty powerful.

When I lost my father in 2010, it shook me to my foundation. Yes, the same foundation of knowing everything is going to be okay. But when I truly examined the emotion I was feeling— no matter how much I missed my father—there was the reality of facing my own mortality. One night shortly after his death, I remember lying in bed and seeing myself from above. I envisioned the view of myself from over our house, then up over the neighborhood, the city, and eventually out into space looking down at how small and insignificant I was. I realized how selfish it is for me to feel deprived and victimized. I'm not the only one who is going through a difficult time, and I am so lucky to have had a father I knew and loved.

Here's something I wrote on my website and posted on July 11, 2010:

I remember the surgeon saying, "It's not good; it is cancer and most likely originated in the lungs…" meaning it has metastasized throughout his body. "All we can do now is pray the Lord has mercy and he doesn't suffer long." The following ten days felt as if I were watching a sad movie. On July 6, my father passed away.

This morning in the shower I was thinking about the moment I heard the surgeon tell us the bad news. It was as if I left my body and God pulled me beside him, with his arm around me, and we had been watching this entire thing together. Then the words came to my consciousness, "It's okay, Jared, I'll take care of him." And I wept…no, I wailed. I wailed till I couldn't catch my breath and

131

wondered if the neighbors could hear me. In that moment I felt the presence of God more than I have in a long time. The saying, "More will be revealed later," became a personal experience.

The last few days it's like a piece of me is missing. Although deep down I know everything is okay, there is a small void. In that moment in the shower I realized its okay to have this void—the missing puzzle piece—and it has a purpose. I felt that God has it in his hand, is smoothing the edges, and will snap it back in when I am ready—and the realization that it will never be back in place totally. Or maybe just a different color... Yes, let's go with that since I don't like the idea of not being whole.

I've been weeping in my dreams, unable to catch my breath, and I wake up. My dreams aren't about my father so much, but there is definitely a sad overtone. I'm not big on dream interpretation—at least not mine—I have enough trouble figuring things out when I'm awake.

I'm reminded of the saying, idea, belief...whatever, that God will only give us as much as we can handle. Whether it's a spiritual experience or our mind's way of dealing with intense emotional states, we are only given as much as we can handle at any given moment. Or maybe that's called shock, I'm not sure. Like when my mother called me the night he passed away and I could hear the paramedics in the background asking questions, I just started shaking. It was weird. I wasn't cold. I was just shaking and started sort of walking around in a daze, a daze that remained until today in the shower.

Even though a piece of me is missing—again—I know it has a purpose. That I have a choice, to let it take me to where I'm supposed to be.

What if you could live a life so perfect and beautiful that you feared neither dying nor living? That you've dealt with those things that cause you regret; they're gone. You've dealt with your fears; they're gone, too. You've accepted yourself for who you are, completely. And as a result, others accept and are drawn to you. You experience love in all its glory.

That life can exist.

I've accomplished it, and so can you.

Acknowledgements

This book has been a true labor of love. A lot of wonderful and amazing people have helped me along the way, certainly more than I've mentioned here. My sincere apologies for anyone omitted.

First, I'd like to thank God, for allowing me to see the miracle in myself and others. Thanks to my beautiful wife Emily, for her relentless support in everything I do (in a box ;-); my mother for being my biggest fan and comforting me—again and again—over the years when I was going through rough times, but most importantly for loving me and herself enough, and having the faith to finally allow me to find my own way regardless of how much she wanted to save me. To my sister Lori, thanks for taking me in so many times when I was failing at life, yet who had the strength to allow me to find my own way. Thank you dad for being such a great provider, I miss you; to Duncan for being such an incredible human being, God put you in my life and showed me the power of vulnerability, love, compassion, perseverance, and action. Thanks to Dallas and Sarah for showing me what mature, loving adults look like, you've brought an entirely different level of enjoyment and perspective to my life; and to Juniper for being so darn cute and reminding me what living in the moment is all about. Thanks to Scott for showing up and letting me know you cared, you're an amazing man and I'm anxious to see what the future holds for you, I know it will be great. Thanks to Robin for helping me see the beauty in unlikely places; to Laura Lake, Justin Lukasavige, Lori Deschene, and Mary Jaksch for taking the time to review my manuscript.

Thank you universe for all the mistakes you allowed me to make and stay alive. It's all gravy.

About The Author

Jared Akers lives in Lee's Summit, MO with his wife Emily and their rescued Westie, *Pepper*. He works full-time as a Senior Search Analyst for a digital marketing agency. He enjoys competing in triathlons' during the summer (at least that was his *latest* obsession at the time of writing this book), spending time with his step-son/daughter, granddaughter, writing about happiness at http://jaredakers.com, and hanging out with his wife. Soon after meeting on February 25, 2007, Jared and Emily become certified SCUBA divers and enjoy traveling to sunny places as much as possible. They also have a podcast, *How to Be Happy with Jared & Emily Akers* which can be found on

Jared's website at: http://jaredakers.com/podcast or on iTunes at http://jaredakers.com/itunes

Contact info: jared@jaredakers.com

Cover design: Lori Akers

Appendix a

Ideal Self Worksheet

To use this worksheet, first write down your ideal self. A good way to think of this is how you would want people to describe you. For example: Rob is a kind, compassionate person who's always on time, witty, hardworking, trusting, works hard, and always makes me feel like I am the most important person in the room. That is, my ideal self is kind, empathetic, funny, hardworking, trustworthy, humble, and a good listener.

My ideal self is_____

_____

_____

_____

_____

Below are two columns. In the left column are emotions that hinder inner-peace and happiness while moving you farther from your ideal self. Any time you're feeling anxious, stressed, or unhappy, go down the list and check off which ones you're feeling.

The right column is the opposing, positive emotions of the left column. When you're feeling something on the left, concentrate, meditate, and focus on the opposing emotion to the right. This exercise will help you move towards your ideal self.

Where Are You?   ## Where You Want To Go

Where Are You?			Where You Want To Go	
Anger	____	→	Self-Control	____
Fear	____	→	Faith	____
Resentment	____	→	Forgiveness	____
Dishonesty	____	→	Honesty	____
Impatience	____	→	Patience	____
Hate	____	→	Love	____
Jealousy	____	→	Trust	____
Envy	____	→	Generosity	____
Laziness	____	→	Activity	____
Procrastination	____	→	Promptness	____
Negative Thinking	____	→	Positive Thinking	____
Self-Pity	____	→	Self-Forgiveness	____
Self-Justification	____	→	Integrity	____
Self-Importance	____	→	Modesty	____
Self-Condemnation	____	→	Self-Esteem	____
Criticizing	____	→	Look For The Good	____
False Pride	____	→	Humility	____

Appendix b

Chapter 6 Actions: Surrender and Letting Go Exercise

This exercise and action is something I learned to be extremely valuable when I first started my journey towards happiness. Being able to take some sort of action is extremely important, besides just sitting there, allowing these things to brew in our heads and torment us.

I use this technique for things that keep me up at night. If I'm sitting there stewing over these things in bed and just can't get to sleep, I get up and take some action. 99% of the time this only takes a few minutes and then I can go back to bed knowing I've taken some action.

The concept is fairly easy as stated in chapter 6, but I've added a new action here. I've used something I call a God box, but you can call it anything you want. It can be a shoebox, recipe card box, or some ornate wooden treasure chest; it doesn't matter. Preferably it should be something you can't open easily. Maybe something simple like wrapping duct tape around a shoe box several times and cut a slit in the top of it.

The concept for this exercise is simple. You write something down and ask yourself if there's something you can do about it. If the answer is yes, you take action, if the answer is no, you put that piece of paper in your box and let it go.

Set a date in the future or once a year (I like just before the New Year). Open your box and see what's inside. You'll be amazed at how some of the seemingly huge ordeals in your life simply melted away. Most likely you'll find it hard to believe you lost any sleep over them at all. In many cases, you might not even remember it!

To make it easier for you, the next page is something you can copy and print off if you like, or just make your own or write in this book.

The instructions are simple.

1. Right your issue down.
2. Circle either *Yes* or *No* answering the question, *Can you do something about it right now, tomorrow, or next week?*
3. If the answer is "Yes," fill in the blanks
4. If the answer is "No," put in your God box.

Issue_____

Can You Do Something About it Right Now,
Tomorrow, or Next Week?   Yes/No

If Yes: What action can you take today, tomorrow, or in
the next week and is there any help our resources you
need to make that happen?

_____

_____

If No: Goes in God box

_____

Issue _____

Can You Do Something About it Right Now,
Tomorrow, or Next Week?   Yes/No

If Yes: What action can you take today, tomorrow, or in
the next week and is there any help our resources you
need to make that happen?

_____

_____

If No: Goes in God box

_____

Issue_____

Can You Do Something About it Right Now,
Tomorrow, or Next Week?   Yes/No

If Yes: What action can you take today, tomorrow, or in
the next week and is there any help our resources you
need to make that happen?

_____

_____

If No: Goes in God box

_____

Issue_____

Can You Do Something About it Right Now,
Tomorrow, or Next Week?   Yes/No

If Yes: What action can you take today, tomorrow, or in the next week and is there any help our resources you need to make that happen?

_____

_____

If No: Goes in God box

13232172R00097

Made in the USA
Charleston, SC
25 June 2012